PRAISE FOR

MINDFULNESS *is better than* CHOCOLATE

"David Michie demonstrates a fine knack for capturing the essence of this important topic and presenting it in a fun and accessible way. In *Mindfulness is Better than Chocolate* he perfectly explains what mindfulness is, why it's important, and, most notably, how we can practice and integrate it into our lives. I know for a fact that mindfulness can enhance health and happiness; this book will help any reader become more mindful."

DR. TIMOTHY SHARP, The Happiness Institute

"A delightful read, providing practical tools and examples around mindfulness and meditation; steeped in tradition, yet brought to life in the modern world. The topic is supported with considerable research examples which resonate with me as a practitioner in the field of positive psychology and it was a joy to see it done so clearly."

SUE LANGLEY, Emotional Intelligence Worldwide

"A fascinating and illuminating journey into the many rewards that practicing mindfulness can bring, from stress release, to greater focus, to a deeper understanding of your own mind."

BETH PHELAN, World Happiness Forum

"A practical and informed exposition of meditative techniques, complemented by a lucid scientific overview."

GORDON PARKER AO, Scientia Professor of Psychiatry,
University of New South Wales

"Essential reading for leaders who want to train their minds to engage in strategic thought."

EMERITUS PROFESSOR GARY MARTIN, CEO,
Australian Institute of Management WA

Also by David Michie

Buddhism for Busy People
Hurry Up and Meditate
Enlightenment To Go
The Dalai Lama's Cat
The Art of Purring
The Magician of Lhasa

DAVID MICHIE

MINDFULNESS
is better than
CHOCOLATE

A PRACTICAL GUIDE TO ENHANCED
FOCUS AND LASTING HAPPINESS IN A
WORLD OF DISTRACTIONS

THE EXPERIMENT
NEW YORK

The Experiment, LLC
220 East 23rd Street, Suite 301
New York, NY 10010-4674
www.theexperimentpublishing.com

This book contains the opinions and ideas of its author. It is intended to provide helpful and informative material on the subjects addressed in the book. It is sold with the understanding that the author and publisher are not engaged in rendering medical, health, or any other kind of personal professional services in the book. The author and publisher specifically disclaim all responsibility for any liability, loss, or risk—personal or otherwise—that is incurred as a consequence, directly or indirectly, of the use and application of any of the contents of this book.

The Experiment's books are available at special discounts when purchased in bulk for premiums and sales promotions as well as for fund-raising or educational use. For details, contact us at info@theexperimentpublishing.com.

Library of Congress Cataloging-in-Publication Data

Michie, David, author.
 [Why mindfulness is better than chocolate]
 Mindfulness is better than chocolate : a practical guide to enhanced focus and lasting happiness in a world of distractions / David Michie, PhD.
   pages cm
 Revised edition of: Why mindfulness is better than chocolate. 2014.
 Includes bibliographical references and index.
   ISBN 978-1-61519-258-8 (pbk.) -- ISBN 978-1-61519-259-5 (ebook) 1. Meditation--Therapeutic use. 2. Happiness. 3. Peace of mind. 4. Mindfulness-based cognitive therapy. 5. Self-actualization (Psychology) 6. Acceptance and commitment therapy. I. Title.
 BF637.M4M54 2015
 294.3'4435--dc23
                                    2014035611

ISBN 978-1-61519-258-8
Ebook ISBN 978-1-61519-259-5

Cover design by Nita Ybarra
Cover photographs: stones © Sintez/iStock photo.com. chocolate © Viktor Lugovskoy / iStockphoto.com
Author photograph by Susan Cameron
Internal design by Alissa Dinallo

Manufactured in the United States of America
Distributed by Workman Publishing Company, Inc.
Distributed simultaneously in Canada by Thomas Allen & Son Ltd.

First printing October 2014
10 9 8 7 6 5 4 3 2 1

This book is dedicated with heartfelt gratitude to my Dharma teachers: Geshe Acharya Thubten Loden, founder of Australia's Tibetan Buddhist Society; Les Sheehy, director of the Tibetan Buddhist Society in Perth, Western Australia; and the Venerable Acharya Zasep Tulku Rinpoche, founder of Gaden for the West. I can never repay their kindness, and without them this book could never have been written.

Contents

1

Is mindfulness *really* better than chocolate?

All of human unhappiness is due to the inability
to sit still in a room alone.

BLAISE PASCAL

I s mindfulness *really* better than chocolate? Come to think of it, is anything better than chocolate? Or is the title of this book nothing more than a shameless ploy to grab your attention?

As it happens, the idea that mindfulness is better than chocolate is based on compelling research. More than 2,000 people in the United States took part in an innovative study using smartphone technology. Panel members were sent questions at different times of the day and night asking what they were doing, what they were thinking, and how happy they felt.[1]

The analysis, published by Harvard University psychologists Matthew Killingsworth and Daniel Gilbert in *Science* magazine, revealed three important facts. First, people were not thinking about what they were doing 47 percent of the time. Second, people were unhappier when their minds were wandering than when they were not. And third, what people were thinking was a better predictor of their happiness than what they were doing.

The researchers summarized: "A human mind is a wandering mind, and a wandering mind is an unhappy mind. The ability to think about what is not happening is a cognitive achievement that comes at an emotional cost."

Long ago, Buddhists reached much the same conclusion. An ancient tale tells of a novice who asked an enlightened monk to reveal the secret of happiness. The monk told him, "I eat, and I walk and I sleep." When the novice replied that he also did these things, the monk replied, "When I eat, I eat. When I walk, I walk. When I sleep, I sleep."

Buddha and the Harvard Psychology Department are most definitely on the same page when it comes to mindfulness. And the Harvard findings are rich with implications for human behavior.

But what concerns us right now is chocolate.

The study shows we're at our happiest when our mind is not wandering—that is, when we're in a state of mindfulness. But "the nature of people's activities had only a modest impact on whether their minds wandered." It would seem that whether we're washing the dishes or eating the most mouth-wateringly delicious Belgian praline, we're just as likely to have a wandering mind. Eating chocolate is no guarantee that we're thinking about what we're doing.

Which is why mindfulness will always trump chocolate as a means of delivering happiness.

Perhaps not surprisingly, there's one human activity where mindfulness is consistently high: sex. Only 10 percent of people reported their minds wandering during this activity, so if I'd called this book *Mindfulness Is Better Than Sex*, I would have found myself on much shakier ground.

Incidentally, one can't help speculating on what those 10 percent of people who reported wandering minds during sex were actually thinking about. Could the old cliché of grocery lists be true? More research, please!

I will admit, however, to being a little mischievous in creating a false dichotomy between mindfulness and chocolate. There's no reason to choose between the two. On the contrary, the highlight of my mindfulness seminars is often an exercise I call "the Lindt technique," in which I invite participants to mindfully enjoy a Lindt chocolate. Their instructions are to focus exclusively on the sensation of eating a chocolate, every element in forensic detail, from opening the foil wrapper to the appearance and heft of the sphere, the explosion of delicious flavors, and savoring the smooth, liquid heart of the chocolate as it bursts in the mouth.

Are you salivating yet?

For two or three minutes a blissful silence ensues. Mindfulness applied to the eating of chocolate—*there's* something that can give even the proverbial grocery lists a run for their money!

Mindfulness in the mainstream

Both mindfulness and meditation have become very fashionable of late. Just as the cheesecloth and hashish brigade of the 1970s have long since matured to become pillars of the establishment, so too has our understanding of meditation evolved in recent decades from hippie-trippy mysticism to mainstream practice.

Although the difference between meditation and mindfulness will be described in more detail later, at the outset it's important to note the distinction between the two words. When we're being *mindful*, we're paying attention to the present moment, deliberately and non-judgementally. When we're *meditating*, we're being mindful of a specific object—such as the sensation of the breath at the tip of our nostrils—for a sustained period of time. Meditation is, if you like, the training ground for mindfulness. Regular meditation enhances our ability to be mindful. We can all enjoy mindfully drinking a cup of coffee without the benefit of meditation practice, but our capacity for mindfulness is greatly enhanced if we meditate regularly.

Doctors these days are as likely to recommend meditation for stress management as they are to prescribe medication. Many of the world's highest profile consumer companies, such as Google, Apple, Facebook, and Twitter, actively support meditation in their workplaces, as do some of the largest financial institutions, accounting firms, manufacturers, and other corporations. No best practice management school is complete these days without a mindful leadership program. The world's most elite athletes, sports stars, and performing artists employ techniques borrowed from the mindfulness toolbox. Mindfulness is a foundation practice across the increasingly popular practices of yoga, tai chi, and a variety of martial arts. Meditation programs have been shown to be among the most successfully deployed programs in prisons to reduce re-offense rates. A wave of research since the turn of the millenium at laboratories in California, New England, Europe, and Australia is focusing on the emerging discipline of contemplative neuroscience. Even the U.S. Marines have got in on the act, coaching soldiers in meditation-based exercises before deploying them in the world's most dangerous war zones.

Mindfulness practices are millennia old, originating in eastern traditions, notably Buddhism, which has extensively practiced, debated, documented, and taught a range of techniques for a variety of purposes. Given that Buddhism has at its heart a reverence for all forms of life, the idea of teaching meditation to soldiers about to parachute into battle may well raise the eyebrows of some. But in describing the exercise as "like doing push-ups for the brain," the U.S. Army general responsible pithily summarized the way meditation has been reframed: just as a healthy body demands regular exercise, goes this paradigm, a healthy mind requires the same.[2]

This move to the mainstream has inevitably been accompanied by a flurry of books. Without any particular plan to build a library on the subject, I have on my personal bookshelves alone a section of books on mindfulness and meditation about three feet long, picked up here and there in recent years. These books espouse a variety of approaches ranging from the determinedly practical to the quirkily esoteric.

Books I *don't* have on my shelves include those by an ever-expanding group of self-styled teachers and mindfulness gurus who go to quite some lengths in the pursuit of mystification. A liberal sprinkling of ™ and © signs is usually warning enough. The requirement to spend large sums of money on weekend intensives should also cause the brow to wrinkle. For the truth is that mindfulness is a simple subject—difficult to practice, no question, but straight-forward to explain.

Given all this, does the world need yet another book on mindfulness?

Some months ago I was delivering a mindfulness seminar to a group of engineers at a business school. The participants were an engaged bunch, and a meditation exercise was followed by a lively Q&A session, during which I was asked: "Why do Buddhist monks meditate? After all, they don't have any stress. All they have to do is hang around for the next meal to arrive."

On the surface of things, this is perhaps a reasonable question. And going by the smiles and nodding, it was clear that this observation chimed with quite a few others in the room. If we assume for a moment that the questioner was essentially correct, and that the life of a Buddhist monk is one long picnic waiting for the next course to be served, it may indeed seem mystifying why stress management would be called for.

But for me the question really summed up the tragically diminished idea many people have of what mindfulness and meditation are all about. Yes, they're great for managing stress, but that isn't why Buddhists do them. Stress management isn't the main reason, nor even a particularly important part of our motivation. To put things in a current, western perspective, it was as if my questioner was asking why people who aren't on Facebook bother with internet access. Why else would you want to go online?

I felt the need to write this book because I'd like to share the *real* treasure of mindfulness—its truly transformative power, the authentic reason Buddhist monks meditate. This explanation is left behind, overlooked, dumbed down, or never even explored by some contemporary mindfulness teachers— and not necessarily with bad intentions. Mindfulness Lite is an easier sell to a wide audience, and can't the world use as many mindful people as possible, albeit of the "push-ups for the brain" variety? Besides, the benefits of meditation are so numerous and now so well established by researchers that you don't need to take people too far along the journey for them to start noticing the favorable physical and psychological effects, so why go further?

At the heart of this reluctance to venture into the heartland of meditation, I'm guessing, is also a certain fear. When people are given the tools to observe the true nature of their own minds for themselves, the experience is a subtle but inevitable game-changer. When the rug is well and truly pulled out from beneath the confection of the "self" we have come to believe ourselves to be, we can never experience ourselves in quite the same way again. Like being able to see the alternative perspective in one of those famous optical illusions, we can never go back to our former innocence. Our view of our "self" changes forever.

East and West

In writing this book, I'm doing so not as a Buddhist monk— tempting though the prospect of a lifetime's free catering may be—nor as someone claiming any preternatural mental abilities. The prosaic truth is that I'm a regular middle-aged corporate consultant with many of the usual personal, business, and financial responsibilities. In the midst of this typically busy twenty-first-century life, I have nevertheless found, in meditation and mindfulness, practices that have transformed my experience of reality dramatically for the better. And I know from talking to other meditators that it's the same for them, too.

My own meditation journey has been informed by Tibetan Buddhism, in particular the lineage established in Australia by the pre-eminent Geshe Acharya Thubten Loden and, more directly, through the teachings I've received from my kind and precious teacher, Les Sheehy. While the knowledge and experience I have acquired has been guided by them, any failure in my attempt to pass on their profound wisdom is very much my own doing.

While I will refer to Buddhist sources and insights where relevant, it's important to note that the study of our own minds isn't about theory or belief. It's about seeing what's there for ourselves. I'll also refer to research from scientific endeavors in fields as varied as psychology, neuroscience, medicine, genetics, and quantum physics.

One of the joys of being alive in the early part of the twenty-first century is witnessing the convergence of so many different dynamics—ancient and contemporary, outer and inner, eastern and western—in arriving at a holistic understanding of consciousness.

For some people, the proliferation of empirical studies showing the benefits of mindfulness encourages personal exploration. Others have a more intuitive understanding of the value of this practice. I hope in this book to share ideas that will inspire both intuitive and analytical thinkers, both left-brain and right-brain thinkers.

I have also intentionally interwoven chapters on mindfulness theory with those explaining how to practice meditation. As fascinating as concepts of mindfulness are, the only way they can have a powerful personal impact is if we apply them. Ideas, theories, and evidence only get us so far. Then we need to move beyond concept.

In my previous nonfiction books, *Buddhism for Busy People*, *Hurry Up and Meditate*, and *Enlightenment to Go*,

I've shared some of the experiences of my own journey, and I do so in this book, too. This isn't because I'm the repository of especially arcane insights, but because I hope you'll find in this more personal account—rather than a straightforward exposition of the subject—themes and discoveries you can relate to, landmarks that may be useful in your own exploration of the mind.

An outline of the mindfulness journey

We begin our exploration with the nuts and bolts of mindfulness—what it is, why it works and how we can benefit from it in basic but profound ways. Stress management? Certainly! Boosting our immune systems and pushing back our biological clocks? That too! The physical and psychological benefits of mindfulness, even if taken no further than this, are well worth getting out of bed ten minutes earlier every morning.

We then move onto the possibilities offered by mindfulness in changing the content of your ongoing conversation with yourself. Chatter, chatter, chatter. We're all up to it. But are there recurring themes in this constant stream of self-talk that don't serve you well? For example, are you a worrier, constantly anticipating all the things that could possibly go wrong then convincing yourself that the worst outcome is almost certain? Or are you a victim, feeling you can never make any headway because of your circumstances, past events, or the people in your life? Or are you someone who struggles to find any compelling purpose or happiness beyond filling your days with as many pleasurable distractions as possible?

The combination of mindfulness with what has become known as cognitive behavior training is one of the most powerful transformation modalities. Creating space amid all the mental agitation, discovering that we can become the observers of our thoughts rather than their unwitting slaves—this is another extraordinary consequence of a more mindful life. It's a consequence that allows us to get proactive about what goes on in our mind, take charge of our own mental trajectories, and thereby exercise choice over the destinies to which our every thought propels us.

The main event—mind itself

And then we come to mind itself. What it is. What it is not. We're no longer doing push-ups here—we're onto something much more exciting! I'll guide you through the practical steps by which you can experience your own mind for yourself, not as a concept or intellectual idea, but directly and first-hand. You'll be empowered to experience the nature of your own consciousness, and if you're anything like most people who've never tried this before, you'll find, in those first glimpses of the pure nature of your own mind, an extraordinary truth. You'll see for yourself how your mind is, quite literally, infinite. How it has no beginning and no end. How, far from being some existential void, it's imbued with the most profound happiness-giving qualities.

You'll experience the paradox that even though you set out to explore your mind, the result is as much a feeling as it is a perception. It's an experience beyond concept and for which words are therefore wholly inadequate, but that may be hinted at using such terms as "oceanic tranquillity" and "radiant love."

Even the briefest encounter with this state is life-changing, because when we can free ourselves from the agitation or dullness that pervades our minds and encounter our own true natures, if only momentarily, we can never go back to believing ourselves to be nothing more than a bag of bones. We have experienced a dimension of being that transcends all our usual ideas of self.

We have come home.

When we begin to explore our own mind, we usually do so for reasons of self-discovery. But an interesting thing happens, because in experiencing our own true nature, we come to recognize that just as we are, others are, too. Our everyday experience of people is one in which we habitually observe and judge based on what we see, at a conventional level, as their apparent characteristics.

Discovering that these characteristics are, ultimately, as temporary and insignificant as our own, a shift occurs. Others may continue the way they've always seemed to be, but now *we* know better. Aware of the more important way in which they exist, as well as the difficulties and challenges they must inevitably endure because of their profoundly self-limiting beliefs, our compassion quite naturally arises. Mindfulness is no longer just about "me." It becomes panoramic.

I can think of nothing more enduringly fascinating or life-enhancing than the practice of mindfulness. No matter where you are on your own journey, I hope you find in this book fresh insights and inspiration to encourage your further exploration. In particular, it's my heartfelt wish that you may abide, however fleetingly, in your own unobstructed mind. For there you'll discover that your own true nature is one of timeless and transcendental bliss.

Chocolate, schmocolate. Show me the meditation cushion!

2

What is mindfulness
and why does it matter?

....

Question: Where's the best place to hide
something of great value?
Answer: The present moment. No one will
ever find it!

YOGA JOKE

....

How easy is it being you?

I often begin meditation seminars by asking this question, and it invariably prompts some rueful smiles, expressions revealing that, for many of us, life is a variation on similar themes. Never before have we felt that we have to work such long hours so relentlessly under so much pressure. The competing demands of all-consuming workplaces, growing children, burdensome financial commitments, aging parents, and lengthening commutes are more wearying than we can remember.

And increasingly there's no respite. The online world, once confined to our desktops, is now in our pockets. Bosses, clients, and numberless others can and do message us at all hours expecting replies. Personal time and vacations are no longer sacrosanct. Formerly enjoyable "downtime" occasions such as dining out or weekend barbecues somehow lose their luster when our fellow diners constantly glance at their phones in case they're missing out on greater excitement elsewhere.

Waking to the shrill call of the alarm at 6 a.m., we intuitively know we shouldn't be checking for messages and updates before we're even fully awake. We don't need scientific evidence to prove what we already subjectively experience—that cognitive overload is degrading our attention span as well as our peace of mind. But still we do it, driven by the imperatives of our job, our friends, or a compulsion we can't even explain.

The reason it's not easy being you may have little to do with frenetic overwork. You may suffer from loneliness, a sense of irrelevance, or despair that whatever you've most sought from life seems to have passed you by. You may be the victim of an injustice that has robbed you of cherished relationships or financial security.

Or maybe there's nothing fundamentally wrong in your world, it's just hard to shrug off the recognition that life hasn't turned out the way you'd hoped. If being truly appreciated for who you really are is a remote prospect, the possibility of deep personal fulfilment may seem unlikelier still.

Stress and dissatisfaction are feelings we generally try to avoid. But here's a paradoxical idea: how about we welcome them? Not so much the negative feelings themselves as an acknowledgement that they exist.

M. Scott Peck began one of the world's most famous self-help classics, *The Road Less Traveled*, with the memorable words "Life is difficult." In so doing, he was echoing the Buddha's very first teaching after attaining enlightenment two and a half millennia earlier, a teaching given only reluctantly, and at the insistence of those around him, because he didn't want to come across as unduly negative when he stated the First Noble Truth: "Dissatisfaction exists."

The point about acknowledgement is that it's the vital first step. There can be no moving on without it. A visit to the doctor begins with a review of symptoms followed by a diagnosis, prognosis, and proposed treatment. These four steps precisely reflect Buddha's Four Noble Truths. Only having acknowledged that there's a problem can we begin our own personal journey of transcendence.[1] This begins when we take our first simple but revolutionary step: we pay attention to the present moment.

The definition of mindfulness

Probably the most widely accepted definition of mindfulness is *paying attention to the present moment deliberately and non-judgementally*. This definition comprises three parts, of which *paying attention to the present moment* is the first.

·········· Paying attention to the present moment . . . ··········

You may respond: what else would I be paying attention to? If I wasn't paying attention to the present moment I'd be incapable of driving the car down the road, sending off emails, preparing gourmet meals, or any of the other activities expected of me on a daily basis.

True enough, but only up to a point. While most of us have a pretty good handle on the here and now, it's often, to borrow from the language of photography, low resolution. When it comes to high resolution we're not so good. We sit on our hotel balcony overlooking a spectacular panorama, but our thoughts are back at the office and a bruising encounter with a colleague. We go for a walk in the park, and far from being absorbed by the wonders of nature, we find ourselves planning next weekend. As the smartphone survey referred to in the previous chapter showed, about half the time we're thinking about something other than what we're actually doing.

Some neuroscientists label this the "narrative" state as opposed to the "direct" state, which is when we're attending *directly* to our senses. The narrative state includes everything in our inner monologue, which begins from the moment we wake up and continues in its desultory fashion throughout the day until we go to sleep. Thoughts, memories, plans, fantasies, all forms of conjecture and speculation, whether creative or humdrum, delightful or debilitating, altruistic or evil—all this mental activity falls into the category of the narrative state.

While no one disputes the importance of thought in planning and so on, our constant absorption in the narrative state is also the cause of much of our unhappiness. "Too much thinking," my teacher Geshe Loden used to say, wagging his finger, "is the main problem."

When we consider the darkest moments of our lives, they're almost always times when we've been trapped in the narrative state: boiling over with anger at the way we have been wronged, filled with despairing thoughts about the end of a relationship, racked with grief at the loss of a loved one, weary with self-loathing. At such times we may wish we could stop thinking about the apparent cause of our unhappiness, but we just seem incapable of it. Trying to focus on something else, after a few moments, and despite our own wishes, we find ourselves once again dwelling on the subject of our unwanted obsession.

Significantly, at such moments the world around us that we can see, hear, smell, taste, and touch may well be neutral or even very pleasant. It's highly likely that we enjoy the kind of material circumstances that most people in the world can only aspire to. If only we could free ourselves from the mad monkey of the mind and "pay attention to the present moment," we could perhaps be free to enjoy these privileged circumstances.

.... *... deliberately ...* ....

Which brings us to the second part of the mindfulness definition. Mindfulness is *deliberate*. It's a state we cultivate intentionally. As we've already seen, although sex triggers high levels of "paying attention to the present moment," most other activities—even the delectation of chocolate—will usually attract our attention for only so long before we're tripping away again in our world of thought.

Some activities seem especially well suited to mindfulness practice. These often have a repetitive quality that people find calming or relaxing. Swimming and cycling lend themselves to keeping the mind in the here and now. Gardening, too, which also offers a multiplicity of direct sensory contact with nature. Walking can be used as a meditative practice. The highest performance levels in sports and the performing arts all demand very high levels of mindfulness. As Justin Langer, one of Australian cricket's greatest all-time opening batsmen and an advocate of meditation, has observed, you can't allow what is written about you in the daily newspapers to impinge on your thoughts for even an instant when you're standing at the wicket preparing for the next ball.

For most beginners, mindfulness is a practice that needs to be assigned to certain activities during the day. Some things we do may lend themselves quite readily to its practice. In time, once we've developed our mindfulness muscles, much more of our lives will be lived more mindfully. But to begin with, we need to cultivate its practice deliberately.

. . . and non-judgementally

The third part of the mindfulness definition is about being non-judgemental. Having intentionally switched to "direct" mode, our challenge is to experience whatever is presented through the doors of our senses without any of the analysis, comparisons, and ruminations that usually accompany sensory experiences and that draw us back into narrative mode so subtly we don't even notice.

Most of us depend on our well-developed critical faculty to manage our busy lives. Moment by moment we're judging, reviewing options, and making choices, whether we're searching the net, talking to friends, hard at work, or walking through the streets. As a result, it's actually quite hard for us simply to experience something without making a judgement about it. The judgement referred to here is not a moralistic one, by the way. It could be as simple as "this coffee is a bit cold" or as cerebral as "use of the word 'rumination' in the last paragraph made me think of cows."

Learning to disengage this constant mental commentary is our greatest challenge when practicing mindfulness. It's just so habitual. We can't help ourselves rushing to judgement, even when enjoying such simple pleasures as eating chocolate. After taking a group through "the Lindt technique" (see Chapter 1) during a seminar, I asked the meditators how it had been for them. One lady explained how frustrated she'd been. Usually she ate her chocolate in two bites, but felt that for the purposes of this exercise it should be a singular experience, so had popped the whole ball in her mouth. She then found it too unwieldy to enjoy as she usually did. As she tried to get comfortable rolling the chocolate around her mouth, she thought how it would have been better if she'd adopted her standard two-bite process. She chastised herself for not doing so.

On a different occasion, a meditator in a corporate group reported how a simple breath-focused meditation we'd just completed, which usually leaves people feeling calmer and more relaxed, had stirred up concerns. About halfway through the session he realized his breathing was fairly shallow and he remembered reading somewhere that taking deep breaths is good for relaxing. He spent the rest of the session worrying if he should be breathing more deeply.

In both cases I hadn't given instructions on how chocolates were to be eaten or breaths breathed because it really didn't matter. All that mattered was being mindful of the experience itself. What tripped those two practitioners of mindfulness up, as it trips us all up, is the difficulty of experiencing anything without judging it.

Meditation and mindfulness— how are they related?

If mindfulness is paying attention to the present moment deliberately and non-judgementally, how do we define meditation? The answer to this question depends on the purpose to which meditation is being put, but perhaps the most practical definition of meditation is *the practice of mindfulness in relation to a specific object over a sustained period of time.*

If you were to ask a room of thirty people to practice mindfulness for a minute, and then asked them what they'd been mindful of, chances are you'd get a variety of answers, ranging from mindfulness of ambient noise, such as birdsong or traffic, to mindfulness of the decor in a room, the sensation of the breeze blowing through the window, or the inhaling and exhaling of breath—or all of the above at various times during the sixty-second period. Any of these answers would constitute a valid mindfulness experience.

When we meditate, we choose an object of meditation and try to stick with it. That object may be physical, such as a flower, a shell, or a statue. Very commonly it's a specific aspect of breathing, such as the sensation of our breath at the tip of the nostrils as we inhale or exhale. Or the object could be a particular visualisation, mantra, or even mind itself—there's a lot more on that in Chapter 11.

The regular practice of meditation supports our development of mindfulness. When we train ourselves to pay attention to just one thing during our ten minutes of meditation each day, we're developing a highly transferable skill. We're also getting better at paying attention to the person sitting across the table from us, or eating the chocolate bar more mindfully, or enjoying the sun on our backs as we walk across the park on a warm summer's morning.

Improved concentration is one significant way meditation enhances our practice of mindfulness. But it's also the case that when we meditate regularly and become more familiar with being in direct mode, we're also more likely to switch back into it deliberately at different times of the day. We may choose to enjoy our morning shower rather than spend it rerunning a futile argument we had the night before. We may forgo the car radio for silence on the drive home from work, paying attention to the here and now, creating space in a frenetic schedule. As we become aware just how much the narrative state dominates our mind and how poorly it often serves us, we find ourselves wishing more and more to let go. Simply to be.

Meditation is a bit like the term "sport" in that it encompasses a fairly wide range of activities. A professional golfer may appear to have little in common with an Olympic swimmer or a soccer player, but all are sportspeople. And when you strip away the apparent differences, you discover more commonality than may at first be apparent. All require cardiovascular stamina, specific muscle training and coordination, and the high levels of emotional intelligence demanded by constant training.

In the same way, a procession of people walking slowly in single file may seem to have little in common with a group of people sitting cross-legged on cushions murmuring mantras or lying on their backs with their eyes open, but all could be engaged in various types of meditation. And when we go beyond surface appearances, we find the same essential requirements for mindfulness and awareness, not to mention the same high levels of emotional intelligence. Apart from being specific about the object of meditation, whatever that may be, we also attempt to focus our attention on that object for a particular period of time.

The similarities between training body and mind are worth exploring. Because we westerners are so culturally fixated on the external, prod-able world, the process of physical training provides some useful metaphors for mental development. This includes the relationship between mindfulness and meditation, which is sometimes blurred.

How meditation supports a mindful life

As a regular gym-goer—I wouldn't go so far as to say "enthusiast"—my personal experience as well as observation of others tells me that most of the soaked-shirt brigade do not have some chromosomal quirk that draws them to treadmills like moths to a lamp. They are there typically because they choose to get fit, burn off excess carbs, lose weight, or age well. In some cases they arrive on medical advice, having faced an existential crisis. Others, less dramatically, arrive at the same point on their own.

While at the gym, we focus on our chosen class or program, encouraged by our trainer to constantly improve. Little by little we may add weights, repetitions, or minutes on a machine. If we can keep up the discipline for a few months, we detect meaningful changes and are encouraged to do more. Although the mechanics of what we do at the gym are our main concern, in reality we're mostly doing it for the twenty-three hours a day we're not at the gym. We may monitor our regime with keen attention, but the main benefit is that our improved cardiovascular fitness, capacity for weight-bearing, and flexibility mean we can cope with much greater ease with whatever life hands us.

Precisely the same applies to the practice of meditation.

We may begin on the recommendation of a doctor, or in seeking our own solution to stress, depression, or anxiety, or in response to a more general wish to enjoy greater mental well-being. If we can keep up the practice for a couple of months, encouraged by our teacher, we'll inevitably experience the benefits. And while we may monitor our regime according to the minutes we spend on it each day, the types of meditation in which we engage and/or our subjective experience while doing it, the real benefit is in the twenty-three hours and fifty minutes a day we're *not* meditating. It allows us to deal with life's inevitable ups and downs with greater mindfulness, along with providing associated benefits—equanimity, inner peace, spontaneity, and zest for life, to name just a few.

Regular meditation therefore supports a more mindful life in the same way a gym routine supports a fitter life. We can practice mindfulness without meditating regularly, just as we can try to get fit through incidental exercise. But it seems a bit pointless. For the sake of just ten minutes a day we might as well benefit from a daily meditation session.

"Ah, but I don't have time," people sometimes say. If that thought just crossed your mind, here's a question: if, by meditating regularly, you knew that at the end of a three-month period you'd receive a massive multimillion-dollar prize, would you somehow be able to find ten minutes each day? So how much is it really about time versus willingness?

With the motivation to meditate in mind, in Chapter 4 I've outlined some of the proven benefits of mindfulness and meditation established by recent clinical studies. Their systemic impacts on body and mind are so powerful, so beneficial, and so profoundly life-enhancing that if you're not already a regular meditator, I hope you soon will be!

But before we get there, how exactly do you meditate?

3

How to meditate

....

The root of "spirit" is the Latin *spirare*, to breathe.
Whatever lives on the breath, then, must have
its spiritual dimension . . .

JANE HIRSHFIELD[1]

....

There are many different meditation methods, but we have to choose one of them to begin with. I'd like to introduce you to what's probably the most widely practiced meditation method in the world: breath-based meditation. Not only is this a simple and powerful way to cultivate the many benefits of meditation, it's also a useful foundation for a more advanced practice that I'll share with you in Chapter 11. Buddha himself called breath-based meditation "an ambrosial dwelling." The accuracy of this wonderfully lyrical description may seem questionable when you start your practice, but have no doubt—it can become true for you, too.

A different metaphor you may find helpful is that of riding a horse, with awareness likened to the rider and the horse the breath. The objective is to sustain a stable union between the two throughout the session.

I'll explain two different kinds of breath-based meditation: breath-counting and nine-cycle breathing meditation. Try each of them out and see which one appeals to you more. If you'd like a guided, ten-minute version of each, you can download them for free from my website, www.davidmichie.com.

How to adopt the best physical posture

To begin, you need to adopt the most conducive physical posture.

1 *Sit with your back straight*. This is the most important element. The freeway of the central nervous system runs inside the spine, and keeping it clear of gridlocks is our prime objective. Whether you sit cross-legged on a cushion on the floor or in a chair the usual western way is up to you.

If you're in a chair, plant your feet solidly on the ground and try to leave them in that position for the whole session. If the chair is a bit high, crossing your legs at the ankles may be a more comfortable posture.

If you're on a cushion, you may find it useful to put it on top of a mat or rug, so that your knees and feet don't press into the hard floor.

On meditation retreats I'm always amazed by the configuration of cushions, blankets, hot water bottles, microwavable beanbags and other nesting materials used by my fellow meditators. If you're a ten-minute-a-day beginner it's unlikely you'll require anything quite so elaborate. But the point is, feel free to do whatever it takes to achieve a sustainable posture where your spine is neither slumped nor artificially stretched, but straight and relaxed.

2 *Rest your hands in your lap*. The usual position is palms facing up, like a pair of shells, the right on top of the left, and tips of the thumbs touching. If you prefer resting your hands palm down on each knee, with your forefingers and thumbs forming a circle, that's fine, too.

3 *Relax your shoulders*. Ideally they should be slightly rolled back, down, and level. Keep your arms comfortably by your sides, not held in tightly.

4 *Adjust the tilt of your head to your current state of mind*. If your mind is highly active, tilt your head down a bit—it can help calm things down. On the other hand, if you're tending towards drowsiness, keep facing straight ahead.

5 *Close your eyes and relax your face*. You'll discover no shortage of inner distractions without adding external stimuli too, so to begin with it's best to shut these off by closing your eyes.

Relax your face—make sure you don't have a clenched jaw or lined forehead. By placing the tip of your tongue behind your front teeth, you can help control the build-up of saliva.

How to adopt the best psychological posture

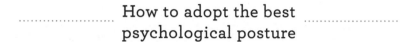

Once you're in the most conducive physical posture, you need to do the same psychologically. Begin by giving yourself permission not to have to think about any of the things that have been occupying your mind until now. The next ten minutes is time out from all your usual preoccupations—you have the other twenty-three hours and fifty minutes of the day for those. As far as possible, try to enjoy pure consciousness of this present moment, without thoughts of the past, the future, or anything else.

You may find it useful to take a few deep breaths and, as you exhale physically, also let go psychologically of previous thoughts. Abide simply in the here and now.

Having drawn a line between the past and this present period of meditation, it's helpful to begin each session with a clear statement of intent. The following affirmation encapsulates what you're wishing to achieve from your meditation practice in a way that's meaningful to you. I suggest you repeat it two or three times:

By the practice of this meditation
I am becoming calm and relaxed,
Happier and more efficient in all that I do,
Both for my own sake as well as for others.

In Tibetan Buddhism, we typically begin each meditation with the following:

To the Buddha, Dharma, and Sangha,
I go for refuge until becoming enlightened.
By the practice of giving and so on,
May I attain enlightenment to benefit all beings.

The meaning of this verse is so profound that a full explanation would require an entire book of its own. In a nutshell, it affirms the direction set by Buddha, his teachings (Dharma), and advanced practitioners on the path (Sangha), with the wish to become enlightened for the benefit of all living beings, also known as *bodhichitta* (literally "the mind of enlightenment"). There's no motivation higher than *bodhichitta*, so if this verse resonates with you, I encourage you to use it.

On the other hand, if you wish to create your own affirmation, the guidelines are to state it in the present, not the future tense; to focus on the positives you wish to achieve, not the negatives you wish to avoid; and to include the well-being of others in your overall objective.

You're now ready to begin meditation practice.

I've set out each of the two breath-based meditation methods below. Within the course of a single session, it's important to stick to one particular meditation method rather than jump around between different types: avoid the mind's habitual tendency to wander.

How to do breath-counting meditation

Place the focus of your attention at the tip of your nostrils and observe the flow of air as you breathe in and then out. Don't focus on any other element of breathing, such as the rise and fall of your rib cage or the sensation of the air flowing through your throat. Rather, remain like a sentry in a gatehouse observing the passage of visitors in and out. That's your only job.

As you breathe out, count "one" in your mind, then on the next out-breath "two," then "three" and "four." Then begin counting at "one" again.

Some meditation teachers suggest you attempt counting your breath up to ten or even twenty-one, but I find that most beginners can't reach ten without losing count—there's too much going on in their minds. If you can get through a whole ten-minute session counting to four without too many concentration problems, it's time to stretch yourself. Next meditation set seven as your count. Then ten and so on, progressively up to twenty-one.

Once you can do that, you'll probably find, quite naturally, that you want to extend your ten-minute session to one that's a little longer. Your concentration is improving (see Chapter 8).

How to do nine-cycle breathing meditation

Focus on inhaling through your left nostril and exhaling through your right nostril for three breaths. Then switch the focus to inhaling through your right nostril and exhaling through your left for three breaths. Finally, broaden your attention to inhaling and exhaling through both nostrils to complete the nine-breath cycle.

A variant of this meditation is sometimes used in yoga, where the practice is supported by physically blocking the nostrils with a hand. But the aim of this method is not so much the physical manipulation of breath as placing attention on the inhalation and exhalation of breath through each nostril. You may continue to breathe through both nostrils, but you are placing all your attention on only one at a time.

Some newcomers to meditation prefer this breath-based method to breath counting because it's somewhat busier. If one of your nostrils is blocked, perhaps because of a cold or sinusitis, you'd be better off using the breath-counting method.

Whichever breath-based meditation you use, as you get further into each meditation session, try to pay more concentrated attention to the detail of your practice: the subtle physical sensation at the tip of your nostrils as you breathe, the coolness of the air coming in, the warmer sensation as you exhale. You can note the start of each in-breath, how it builds up, then how it tapers; the gap between in- and out-breaths; then the start, middle, and fading away of each exhalation; and the much longer gap at the end of each exhalation.

As you progress into a meditation session, your breathing and other elements of your metabolism quite naturally slow down. You'll become more and more conscious of the gaps between out-breath and in-breath, and between in-breath and out-breath. In these moments, simply enjoy the temporary absence of all activity, breath, thought, and distraction. As far as possible, try to experience pure presence.

········ How to end your meditation session ··········

How do you know when your ten minutes is up? You can put a watch in a place where you can check it easily by opening your eyes. If the need to check your watch becomes a distraction, however, use the alarm on your mobile phone, placing the phone under a cushion if necessary to avoid an unduly shrill end to your session.

It's useful to close as you began, with the same statement of intent:

> By the practice of this meditation
> I am becoming calm and relaxed,
> Happier and more efficient in all that I do,
> Both for my own sake as well as for others.

Or alternatively:

> To the Buddha, Dharma, and Sangha,
> I go for refuge until becoming enlightened.
> By the practice of giving and so on,
> May I attain enlightenment to benefit all beings.

So much for the nuts and bolts of meditation. But what about the experiential challenges you're likely to face along the way, and how can you work to overcome them?

How to combat agitation and dullness

The two main obstacles to meditation are agitation and dullness. Each of these exists on a spectrum from gross to subtle.

Gross agitation is what happens when, for example, somewhere between breaths two and three, a snatch of music from a passing car outside reminds us of an event when that same piece of music was playing. Before we know it, we're associating with that moment, perhaps reliving the drama of it before our mind flicks on to a related notion, and within moments we're ten ideas away, lost in the forest of conceptuality. Anywhere between a few seconds and much longer may pass before we suddenly remember "I'm supposed to be meditating!"

With gross agitation, we completely lose the object of meditation. When you recollect that you're trying to meditate, begin counting again at one or start over on the nine cycles.

When you begin meditating, you may experience so much gross agitation that the idea of subtle agitation may seem entirely academic. People typically say, "I try to meditate, but I just can't clear my head of thoughts." But the more you practice, the more you'll find that your agitation morphs into a subtler form. You'll hear the same snatch of music from a passing car, only this time, when you remember the event it evokes, it won't affect your ability to continue paying some attention to breathcounting. You'll continue to count your exhalations while a part of your mind is engaged in the memory—this is *subtle agitation*.

You may succeed in counting many more cycles of four while the subtle agitation continues. More tellingly, you may only realize that the subtle agitation is out of control when you hear yourself exhale "seven"—and you were only supposed to be counting in cycles of four!

Perhaps the most insidious form of subtle agitation is when we find ourselves commentating on the meditation session itself. For example:

One . . .
Two . . .
Well, here we are then. Nice and calm.
Three . . .
Making progress.
Four . . .
Hardly any thoughts at all.

And so on!

Tibetans have a wonderful expression for subtle agitation—"water flowing under ice." I like the phrase because it's such a vivid description of the experience. Little by little, our job is to withdraw our attention from this underlying narrative and ensure that our full attention is focused purely on the chosen object of meditation.

The other meditation obstacle, dullness, occurs when our concentration is threatened by sleepiness. *Gross dullness* is when we discover we've nodded off completely. On meditation retreat, the first post-lunch session of the afternoon is often a time when minds grow dull and postures slide, and it's even been known for snoring to be heard before a neck-snap returns the embarrassed meditator to the here and now.

This is one reason, by the way, that it's useful to call what we do "meditation *practice*." We're not making any claims about being able to meditate. We're merely practicing!

Like subtle agitation, *subtle dullness* doesn't interrupt our ability to focus on the object of meditation, but it's there all the same. Maintaining the clarity of our focus then becomes our main challenge.

When most people start out meditating, they often find they have a tendency to experience one of these two obstacles rather than the other. We should use common sense to try to reduce any external factors. If, for example, we're always overwhelmed with tiredness and we're trying to meditate at 9 p.m. every night, could we move our session to an earlier slot? If dullness is still a problem first thing in the morning, would a shower beforehand help wake us up?

But apart from trying to get our external environment right, there are two meditation tools that are essential to our practice.

How to distinguish between
mindfulness and awareness

Mindfulness in this particular context means remembering the object of meditation. *Awareness* is being aware of what your mind is actually doing.

When I first heard these terms, they sounded very similar, but over time I've come to understand that they're actually quite different. The best illustration I've heard to explain their difference is what happens when you carry a very full mug of coffee across a room. The surface of the liquid near the rim of the mug could easily spill over, so you're watching it with great care. Mindfulness equates to that very close attention you're keeping on the surface of the coffee.

As you carry the mug, however, part of your attention is also taking in the bigger picture, making sure you're not about to trip over the dog or bump your elbow against a doorframe. That part of your attention, the part that's keeping a check on the bigger picture, is awareness. While working towards the same goal as mindfulness, it's nevertheless a slightly different aspect of consciousness.

The key to improving one's meditative concentration can be summed up in just one word: practice. In the words of golfing legend Gary Player, "The harder I practice, the luckier I get." Mindfulness and awareness will only ever be concepts unless we apply them, become familiar with them and discover their value for ourselves. Similarly, agitation and dullness will continue to challenge us, but with effort our concentration evolves to the point that they trouble us less and eventually disappear altogether.

How mindful should you be?

The idea of subduing their own mind can bring out a masochistic streak in some people. You can almost see the steam coming out of their ears as, egged on by the aphorism about subduing oneself being a loftier goal than conquering a thousand times a thousand men in battle, they sit in adversarial readiness for their mind to show the first sign of wavering from their chosen object of meditation.

Willpower and endurance are important qualities when cultivating any new practice-based skill, including meditation. But they must be applied with wisdom and compassion for oneself. For the truth is that learning to meditate is like learning to walk. Crawling babies don't decide one day that enough is enough, it's time to walk, before heaving themselves to their feet and taking their first steps. They'll be lifted by their parents countless times before they can stand upright unaided for just a few seconds. Hundreds of tentative first steps will inevitably end in collapse. A handful of successive steps without falling over is seen as a major breakthrough.

When we see a child fall over every time they try to walk, we don't think of them as a failure. Our only thought is to encourage them to try again, in the knowledge that there'll come a day when they'll not only be able to walk, but also to run, skip, and jump—as long as they keep at it. If they get tired of falling over, we may distract them with some new activity, in the knowledge that we can return to the biped thing when they're feeling refreshed.

So, too, with meditation. Thoughts are going to arise in your mind, just like waves arise in the sea, because that's the mind's nature. You're not a loser because you've tried a hundred times and you still can't go for two minutes without gross agitation. As both science and personal experience attest, the more you stick at it, the better you'll get. One day you'll not only go for two minutes without gross agitation, you'll be able to sit for half an hour without it, abiding in the true nature of your mind, in states approaching tranquillity or even bliss.

The only way to fail is to stop trying. But in doing so, like a child deciding they've fallen over one time too many, we'll be diminishing our own future in ways we can't begin to fathom.

So keep at it, but in a realistic way. Apply your concentration and keep trying, but don't get wound up or stressed out about it. Buddha himself gave some helpful advice on the subject of how best to approach each meditation session. One of his students played the Indian equivalent of the guitar, the vina, before becoming a monk. Using this as a metaphor, Buddha asked him, "How did you get the best sound out of your vina? Was it when the strings were very tight or when they were very loose?"

"Neither. When they had just the right tension, neither too taut nor too slack."

"Well, it's exactly the same with your mind," said Buddha.

How does a breath-based meditation session feel?

The subjective experience of breath-based meditation varies not only from person to person, but also from session to session, depending on what else is going on in your life. Just as those who live by the sea come to know its many "moods," reflected by choppiness, smoothness, darkness, lightness, and myriad shades of blue, so too each meditation is subtly—or sometimes quite markedly—different.

Your experience will also differ within each session. Five whole minutes focusing on the breath can significantly calm an agitated mind. Regrettably, it's also true that a reasonably calm mind, if suddenly struck with the recognition of a missed deadline, may become like a bug trapped in a lampshade.

No matter how much you try to focus on your breath, you keep thinking about your lapse.

Having got those important caveats out of the way, there *are* certain qualities to a typical meditation session. First and most obviously, we become both physically and mentally calmer and more relaxed. This is conducive to equanimity, a state in which we're better able to deal with whatever challenges we face in our lives. Whether processing memories, considering difficult people, or contemplating actions we need to take, we can do so with greater neutrality, acceptance, and calm.

When we focus on our breath, our awareness of impermanence is heightened. As each inhalation begins and builds, and is followed by exhalation, we become more conscious of this process in everything. All is impermanent. The building awareness of this fact, both consciously and subconsciously, helps us let go. Over time we find ourselves feeling less anxious, grasping, needy, or desperate. Whatever we're having to deal with in our lives, this, too, will pass.

Breath by breath in each session, we shift increasingly away from narrative mode to direct mode. Our inner monologue becomes less intrusive and demanding. We're more appreciative just to be in this moment, here and now, without the need for memories, plans, or conjecture. The present moment is the only one that exists, and right now it's a moment of calm contentment. Having created space in our mind, we find we become less reactive. We've opened up the possibility of different ways to respond even to familiar problems or people.

The peacefulness we sense when we meditate is qualitatively different from the way we feel on a drowsy summer's afternoon or after a relaxing glass of wine. Paradoxically, we're also alert. Our awareness is heightened by practice, and leaves us more attentive to people and situations around us.

This combination of relaxation, letting go, equanimity, alertness, and contentment is a short account of the subjective experience of breath-based meditation. But as we'll see in the next chapter, for all the gentleness of this practice, beneath the threshold of our consciousness the impact of mindfulness on both body and mind are profoundly life-changing.

Meditation checklist

1 *Establish your physical posture.* Your back is straight, your legs are crossed on a cushion or planted on the floor, hands resting like a pair of shells, shoulders rolled back, arms loose by your sides, head tilted according to your state of mind, the tip of your tongue on the roof of the mouth, face relaxed, and eyes shut.

2 *Establish your psychological posture*. Give yourself permission not to think about your usual concerns. The next ten-minute period is time out.

3 *Mentally establish your motivation*. Repeat two or three times either:

By the practice of this meditation
I am becoming calm and relaxed,
Happier and more efficient in all that I do,
Both for my own sake as well as for others.

or:

To the Buddha, Dharma, and Sangha,
I go for refuge until becoming enlightened.
By the practice of giving and so on,
May I attain enlightenment to benefit all beings.

4 *Begin your breath-based meditation session*. Focus on the object of meditation and try to retain this focus without being too uptight or too relaxed about it.

5 *Use mindfulness and awareness*. Remember the object of meditation and keep a watch on what your mind is actually doing. Bring your attention back every time it wanders.

6 *End the session*. However good or bad your concentration during the session, try especially hard to focus strongly at the end—finish like a winner. Afterwards, repeat your affirmation two or three times:

By the practice of this meditation
I am becoming calm and relaxed,
Happier and more efficient in all that I do,
Both for my own sake as well as for others.

or:

To the Buddha, Dharma, and Sangha,
I go for refuge until becoming enlightened.
By the practice of giving and so on,
May I attain enlightenment to benefit all beings.

Allow yourself a few moments to open your eyes and come back to the room.

4

The benefits of meditation and mindfulness

....

Within yourself is a stillness and a sanctuary to which
you can retreat at any time and be yourself.

HERMANN HESSE

....

When my book *Hurry Up and Meditate* was published in 2008, I made the claim that if the benefits of meditation were available in capsule form, it would be the biggest selling drug of all time. This claim was based on an available body of evidence that, though broad and deep, was actually quite limited compared with the burgeoning body of evidence that has developed since.

As the powerful effects of meditation have been validated by all manner of research teams, institutes, and forums, the "biggest selling drug of all time" suggestion has been voiced by a growing chorus of scientists. So dramatically has the study of mindfulness grown over the last ten years that according to one group of specialists, the number of research papers published on it rose from 28 in 2001 to 397 in 2011.[1]

Providing an overview of the benefits of mindfulness has also become a larger and more complex task. Not only have far more studies delivered results showing a multiplicity of benefits to mindfulness, from managing depression to enhancing our enjoyment of music, but our understanding of the way mindfulness works has also evolved, so that defining a particular benefit as "physical" or "psychological" now seems artificial.

Managing high blood pressure may, on the surface of things, be a measurable and purely physical benefit, but it only occurs because of the psychological change that precedes it. Similarly, enhancing the emotional resilience of corporate executives may seem a largely cerebral pay-off, but it will inevitably be accompanied by complex hormonal and other changes, enhancing the immune system, cardiovascular health, and even the aging process of those same executives. The benefits of meditation are holistic, embracing both body and mind: it's a contrivance to divide the two.

This chapter summarizes some of the more important benefits of meditation. It's necessarily in short form rather than detailed, and covers well-established advantages along with several of the more recent findings.

Rather than present benefits in tidy but artificial boxes, I've arranged them across a holistic spectrum, starting with studies that focused mainly on physical outcomes and proceeding to those that were more psychological in orientation. Given the growing importance of mindfulness in the workplace, I've devoted a separate chapter to that, too (see Chapter 5).

Like a box of delicious soft-centered chocolates, some of these benefits will be of more immediate personal interest to you than others. Feel free to riffle through this chapter and savor those of most immediate appeal, leaving the others to come back to sample later on. The footnotes will take you to the original research studies, or books or online articles about them, and support your further exploration of those subjects you find of particular interest.

Meditation reduces stress

Given that stress is endemic in many people's working lives, and that the experience of stress over a sustained period has such wide-ranging and profoundly negative impacts on both body and mind, the value of meditation in reducing stress is a good place to start. Most people can experience at least some of the stress-reducing benefits of meditation directly, immediately, and without any previous experience. A breath-based meditation, like those described in the previous chapter, should see your breathing and heart rate slow down quite noticeably, your blood pressure—if elevated—fall, and your muscles soften.

In short, you relax.

Could you not achieve the same thing by sitting on the sofa with a cup of tea? The difference is that when we meditate, our body is relaxed but our mind is focused—a state of being quite different from our usual "taking it easy" condition.

For more than thirty-five years, Dr. Herbert Benson, director of the Benson-Henry Institute for Mind Body Medicine and an associate professor at Harvard Medical School, has been studying what he calls "the relaxation response," a state elicited by meditation. Importantly, he has described how the relaxation response has impacts that go well beyond any specific meditation session. What's more, practicing meditation over a period of time has significant cumulative benefits.

Research shows that when we meditate there's reduced activity in part of the brain called the amygdala, which governs the feeling of being stressed. The body also produces less cortisol, a stress-related hormone.[2]

Some people have the mistaken idea that feeling stressed can put you into a state where you get things done. In fact, the opposite is the case. In neuroscientific terms, the executive functions of the brain responsible for short-term memory, processing information, knowing what to pay attention to, making decisions, emotional regulation, and prioritizing all benefit from mindfulness training. By contrast, when the amygdala becomes overactive, it hijacks this area of the brain, seriously impairing these functions.

If you've ever been in an argument or other situation where your emotions are deeply engaged, and you simply can't think of a single word to say, you've experienced the effect of an overactive amygdala.

By contrast, when we meditate the amygdala is stood down, the executive functions of the brain thrive, and long after our meditation session has ended, activity in the amygdala is moderated. Confirming Dr. Benson's findings about the enduring impact of meditation, our emotional regulation and ability to manage stress extend well beyond the on-cushion experience. It also changes our off-cushion reality.

Meditation lowers high blood pressure and helps treat heart disease

Researchers Michael Murphy and Steven Donovan were among the first to summarize the findings of literally hundreds of research studies on meditation in their pioneering work *The Physical and Psychological Effects of Meditation*.[3] By far the majority of early studies focused on physiological effects, which were relatively easy to measure. Dozens of studies have demonstrated how meditation lowers blood pressure in people who suffer from high blood pressure (hypertension).

Hypertension is sometimes called "the silent killer" because unless your blood pressure is monitored, you won't even be aware that it's high—until you're in the back of an ambulance being rushed to hospital after a heart attack.

Not only will meditation help manage hypertension, but studies have shown that regular meditation by patients with heart disease can deliver a significant improvement in exercise tolerance and ECG performance.

Meditation also slows down the impact of hardening of the arteries (atherosclerosis) and dilates the arteries, allowing increased blood flow through the body.

While it would be rash to throw out your blood pressure drugs at the start of your meditation journey, over time, and under medical advice, you may discover that they become unnecessary.[4]

Meditation boosts immunity

When we're stressed, our physiological balance shifts into "fight and flight" mode, increasing the production of hormones such as adrenalin. While these are useful in dealing with imminent danger, frequent exposure to low-level stress compromises our immune system. This is because when our bodies are producing adrenalin, they cut down on the production of endorphins, the neurotransmitters needed to protect our bodies against foreign organisms at a cellular level.

It's therefore no accident that we're more likely to fall prey to cold and flu viruses when we're feeling run-down or stressed out. It's also well established that when we meditate, our bodies shift into self-repair mode. Our production of endorphins dramatically increases, as does that of immunity-boosting hormones such as melatonin, a powerful antioxidant that destroys harmful free radicals, which cause such destruction at a cellular level.

Improved immunity helps us combat viruses of all kinds, not just the ones that cause us more trivial problems such as colds and flu. Scientists are only beginning to quantify the impact of meditation on immunity—and the more research that takes place, the more wide-ranging those impacts are found to be.

DHEA (dehydroepiandrosterone), the most abundant steroid in the body and key to immune function, was identified as early as 1968 as increasing significantly with meditation. A number of studies have confirmed its usefulness in combating bacterial, parasitic, and viral infections, including HIV.

Serotonin is another neurotransmitter known to increase with meditation. Serotonin helps regulate mood, appetite, and sleep. While these may not directly impact on the immune response, they play an important support role—higher serotonin levels are associated with promoting wellbeing and happiness.

Anecdotally, my observations of fellow meditators is that they do seem less affected by the illness and lethargy that come with winter. And speaking personally, I used to suffer from flu at least once every winter before I began meditating regularly. Now I hardly ever get colds or flu, and if I do, the symptoms are fairly minor and tend to last only a few days.

While we may think that the most important pharmaceutical manufacturers are to be found in various office parks around the world, in truth they are located inside our own bodies, constantly monitoring and responding to our psycho-physical state. Offer the suggestion of an optimized state of being to these manufacturers, and they'll deliver accordingly.

Meditation slows aging

A growing number of studies reveals the different ways meditation slows the aging process. The Shamatha Project, a comprehensive longitudinal study of intensive meditation undertaken in 2011, followed sixty participants in a meditation retreat guided by meditation teacher and author B. Alan Wallace over three months. A research team led by Dr. Clifford Saron of the University of California Davis Center for Mind and Brain showed that telomerase activity was about 33 percent higher in the white blood cells of meditators than in control groups.[5]

Telomeres are found at the end of each chromosome in our bodies, protecting them from deterioration. When cells divide during the process of genetic copying, a very small portion of the telomere does not get copied. This means that as we age our telomeres get shorter, but telomerase is an enzyme that helps rebuild them.

Dr. Saron observed:

Meditation may improve a person's psychological well-being and in turn these changes are related to telomerase activity in immune cells, which has the potential to promote longevity in those cells. Activities that increase a person's sense of well-being may have a profound effect on the most fundamental aspects of their physiology.[6]

Separately, work undertaken by a team led by Australian Nobel Prize–winning researcher Elizabeth Blackburn has shown that meditation may slow genetic aging and enhance genetic repair.[7] A summary of their work says that "some forms of meditation may have salutary effects on telomere length by reducing cognitive stress and stress arousal and increasing positive states of mind and hormonal factors that may promote telomere maintenance."

These recent studies support much earlier findings by Dr. Robert Keith Wallace, published in the *International Journal of Neuroscience* more than 30 years ago, showing that among subjects with an average chronological age of 50, those who had been practicing transcendental meditation for more than five years had a biological age twelve years younger than their chronological age. In other words, a 55-year-old meditator had the biological markers of a 43-year old.[8]

The role of the hormone DHEA is also part of the aging jigsaw. The only hormone known to decrease directly with age, DHEA protects us from heart disease, helps fight bacteria and viruses, and has powerful anti-inflammatory properties— critical in the prevention of many illnesses including arthritis, osteoporosis, and certain cancers. DHEA also helps prevent progressive atrophy of the thymus gland, a key driver of aging. A variety of studies have investigated the impact of meditation on DHEA. Some have claimed increases in DHEA levels of up to 90 percent within weeks of subjects learning to meditate.[9]

There's a compelling case for meditation even if our focus is purely on disease prevention and physical wellbeing. As these studies show, meditation not only has the potential to enhance the quality of our lives, it may even extend life itself. One day in the not-too-distant-future we may be able to answer definitively the plea "I don't have time to meditate" with the response "You'll have much less time if you don't!"

Meditation reduces health costs

A study of 1,418 people in Quebec, Canada, by Robert Herron and Stephen Hillis showed that after these people started the regular practice of transcendental meditation, their health costs declined by an average of 5–13 percent over a six-year period.[10] Given that such a large proportion of people seek medical help for stress-related conditions, this finding, while significant, should come as no surprise.

If you're wondering why a number of studies refer specifically to transcendental meditation, this is because, as a standardized, secular form of meditation widely practiced in the West, it lends itself especially well to the requirements of scientific study. More recently, other secular forms of meditation, especially mindfulness meditation, have also become more widespread and the subject of numerous research studies. Although transcendental meditation uses a mantra as the object of meditation while mindfulness meditation focuses on mind itself, a recent study suggests no significant difference in impacts between one type of meditation and another. Differences were seen, however, with the amount of meditation practiced, the benefits correlating with time spent meditating.[11]

In short, whatever credible meditation method we choose, the more we practice it, the better we get, and the more powerful the impact on our body–mind continuum.

Meditation helps manage chronic pain

Chronic pain was an early subject of investigation by Jon Kabat-Zinn, perhaps the pre-eminent authority on mindfulness and medicine today. Repeated studies have confirmed Dr. Kabat-Zinn's early findings, published in the *Clinical Journal of Pain* in 1986, showing "large and significant overall improvements" among a sample of 225 chronic pain patients who were taught meditation and followed up between two and a half months and four years later. Dr. Kabat-Zinn wrote:

> *Most subjects reported a high degree of adherence with the meditation techniques, maintenance of improved status over time, and a high degree of importance attributed to the training program. We conclude that such training can have long-term benefit for chronic pain patients.*[12]

Subsequent studies continue to reinforce this finding, including an intriguing one by Dr. Fadel Zeidan and colleagues published in the *Journal of Neuroscience*.[13] What I find particularly interesting about this study is that eighteen "healthy young adults" with no prior meditation experience were taught mindfulness meditation before being subjected to painful heat (120 degrees Farenheit) over parts of their right calf over a period of five minutes. All this occurred while they were inside a magnetic resonance imaging machine (MRI) that was scanning their brain.

The study found that when participants meditated they showed 40 percent lower pain intensity ratings and a 57 percent decline in pain unpleasantness.[14] These impressive results are particularly striking when you consider the inexperience of the meditators. What if they took time to hone their ability? Would the pain intensity decline even more? Other studies showing a definite "dosage effect" of meditation would certainly suggest this. The implications for sufferers of long-term pain of all varieties are both clear and encouraging.

Meditation reduces mortality

We all know we're going to die, but most of us would prefer it not to happen just yet.

Two hundred and two elderly individuals suffering from high blood pressure were taught transcendental meditation, then studied to see what happened in the years that followed. Compared with control samples, the meditators showed a 23 percent decrease in deaths arising from all causes, a 30 percent decrease in the rate of cardiovascular mortality and a 49 percent decrease in the rate of cancer-related mortality. The researchers wrote:

These results suggest that a specific stress-decreasing approach used in the prevention and control of high blood pressure, such as [transcendental meditation], may contribute to decreased mortality from all causes and cardiovascular disease in older subjects who have systemic hypertension.[15]

Other studies also suggest that meditators live longer. An early one, published in the *Journal of Personality and Social Psychology* in 1989, looked at the impact of meditation among the residents of eight residential care homes who had an average age of 81. Residents were assigned to one of three programs—transcendental meditation, active thinking, relaxation—or a control group with no program.

Findings showed that the meditation group improved the most over a range of physical and mental health measures. Intriguingly, after three years all the meditators were still alive, while the survival rate in the control group was 63 percent. Survival rates in the other two groups fell between the two extremes of the control group and the meditators.[16]

Again, quite apart from the many other benefits of meditation, if our only truly finite resource is time, it makes sense to meditate. Mindfulness not only helps us avoid spending time in the mental wastelands of the past and the future, these studies suggest it will also give us, quite simply, more of it.

Meditation helps people suffering from chronic inflammatory conditions

Stress plays a major role in chronic inflammatory conditions such as rheumatoid arthritis, inflammatory bowel disease, and asthma. A study by neuroscientists at the University of Wisconsin–Madison together with the Center for Investigating Healthy Minds in the Waisman Center compared physical therapies, including walking, nutritional changes, and so on, with a mindfulness-based approach. While both techniques were effective in reducing stress, mindfulness was more effective at reducing stress-induced inflammation.

Significant numbers of sufferers of inflammatory conditions experience negative side effects with conventional drugs or just don't respond to them. Melissa Rosenkranz, lead author of the study, observed: "This is not a cure-all, but our study does show that there are specific ways that mindfulness can be beneficial, and that there are specific people who may be more likely to benefit from this approach than other interventions."[17]

Dr. Steven Rosenzweig and colleagues at Drexel University's College of Medicine in Philadelphia have studied the impact of meditation on people with chronic inflammatory conditions. Quoted in an article published by the Arthritis Foundation, Rosenzweig explained:

People diagnosed with arthritis may think their futures are grim, and that their pain will always limit their enjoyment of life. The response of the body is to become tenser. So mindfulness practice allows us to step back from negative thinking. We just come back to the present time, become calmer, and respond by working with the current situation.[18]

He identifies three ways meditation can benefit people suffering from chronic painful conditions. First, the intensity of pain can be lowered. Second, the cycles of pain escalation can be moderated. And third, even if pain is present, it can become less intrusive in one's life and thoughts.

In summary, meditation has a highly positive role both in managing the impact of a chronic inflammatory condition and in helping prevent them getting worse.

Meditation lessens the likelihood
of recurring depression

In their 2007 book *The Mindful Way through Depression: Freeing Yourself from Chronic Unhappiness*, a team of leading scientists—Mark Williams, John Teasdale, Zindel Segal, and Jon Kabat-Zinn—deliver a proven mindfulness program. Meditation as a preventative approach to depression is a concept only a couple of decades old in the West, but is quickly gaining ground, given the prevalence of depression in our society. As anyone who has suffered from depression can tell you—and having been a deeply depressed young man in my twenties I know this all too well—one of the worst things about depression is the way it keeps returning, becoming so ingrained in your thinking you can't imagine ever being truly happy. You feel that you're doomed to be miserable for the rest of your life.

Clinical trials show that mindfulness works as well as antidepressants in preventing the relapse of depression. Mark Williams, professor of clinical psychology at the University of Oxford's Department of Psychiatry, explains how the insula is the part of the brain that enables us to feel deep emotions, including love. A feeling of loss is therefore very real, and because the insula is closely linked to parts of the brain involved in analytical thought, we not only feel bad, we also think about all the reasons why we do. Unhappiness-creating thoughts reinforce negative feelings and the result is a depressing downward spiral. But as Professor Williams explains, "Meditating breaks this cycle by reducing the links between the insula and the parts of the brain that analyze, as we have seen on brain scans."[19]

In neuroscientific terms, by disengaging the insula from the rest of the brain, we stop hurting ourselves with negative thoughts. The Dalai Lama puts this in broader terms when he says that pain is inevitable but suffering is optional. We'll all experience loss, grief, and heartache at some point. But whether or not we keep dwelling on it and torturing ourselves with it is something in which we have a choice—although it may not feel that way at the time.

I discovered only recently that the word "suffer" has a Latin origin meaning "carry." Many people, myself included, have kept on carrying pain long after their initial experience of it. Meditation helps us put it down—and move on. Exactly how this can occur is outlined in much more detail in Chapter 9.

If you're experiencing depression and wish to experiment with meditation, the consistent advice given by medical experts is not to attempt long meditations. Ten-minute sessions are quite sufficient for any newcomer, whatever their state of mind. While meditation can be a life-changing tool, if you're facing serious mental issues it would be best to discuss this practice with an experienced counselor first.

Meditation helps manage
and prevent anxiety

Anxiety and stress are sometimes seen as the same thing, but there is a difference. Stress is a response to a real-life situation—a looming deadline, a physical threat, an unavoidable confrontation—while anxiety arises largely from worry. Feelings of apprehension or fear that arise with anxiety may be specific, but are usually more generalized or even unknown—we may not know *why* we're feeling anxious, which makes us all the more anxious.

Because the brain doesn't distinguish between the real and the imagined, if we have anxiety-creating thoughts, the fight-or-flight response is triggered. Our amygdala closes down the executive functioning of our brain and ramps up the supply of stress-producing cortisol. Paradoxically, this is the last thing we need—now we can't even think straight. An overactive amygdala is one of the classic indicators of anxiety.

The relaxation response created by meditation has the opposite effect. The amygdala is stood down, the body goes into self-repair mode, mood-enhancing chemicals such as serotonin are stimulated, and the executive functions of the brain are fully supported. Meditation gives us the tools both to break out of our anxiety and to establish a state of mind in which we're less likely to experience anxiety.

Clinical tests have shown that meditation is highly effective in helping prevent anxiety and break the cycle of anxiety-creating thoughts. If you'd like to explore this subject further, you may find the book *The Mindful Way Through Anxiety: Break Free from Chronic Worry and Reclaim Your Life*, by Dr. Susan M. Orsillo and Dr. Lizabeth Roemer, a useful resource.

Meditation reduces feelings of loneliness

In our aging society the feeling of loneliness, especially among the elderly, is a growing risk with both psychological and physical consequences. Loneliness has been linked to an increased risk of heart disease, Alzheimer's disease, depression, and premature death.

Researchers at UCLA showed how meditation successfully reduced feelings of loneliness in a group of forty participants aged between 55 and 85. Helping participants be attentive to the present moment instead of living in the past or the future was an important benefit, countering feelings of loneliness.

Not only that, but blood samples taken before and after showed that meditation also reduced the expression of genes and protein markers involved in inflammation—the primary players in many diseases and psychological disorders.[20]

Steve Cole, a professor at the UCLA School of Medicine noted: "Reductions in the expression of inflammation-related genes were particularly significant because inflammation contributes to a wide variety of the health threats including cancer, cardiovascular diseases, and neurodegenerative diseases."[21]

Like depression, loneliness arises from unhappiness-creating thoughts feeding into the insula, deepening the negative spiral of thoughts and feelings. Unhealthy bereavement over the passing of a life partner can fuel this, when the period of natural grieving extends to a recurring and painful sense of loss. Meditation provides the tools not only to abide more comfortably in the present, but also to observe rather than engage with unhappiness-creating thoughts. With experience, this practice strengthens, offering a meditator the freedom to slip free from misery-creating patterns.

In the words of Zen Buddhist teacher Thich Nhat Hanh, "People suffer because they are caught in their views. As soon as we release those views, we are free and we don't suffer anymore."[22]

Meditation promotes good sleep

A recent University of Utah study on the impact of meditation showed the benefits of mindfulness not only on stress management during the day, but also on sleep. According to researcher Holly Rau:

People who reported higher levels of mindfulness described better control over their emotions and behaviors during the day. In addition, higher mindfulness was associated with lower activation at bedtime, which could have benefits for sleep quality and future ability to manage stress.[23]

This finding confirms the results of other research studies showing that meditation helps people get to sleep more easily, sleep for longer, and reduce their use of sleep medication.[24]

Specifically, meditation promotes healthy melatonin levels, which are important for managing stress and getting a good night's sleep. Melatonin helps regulate our circadian rhythms—it's often prescribed by doctors because it's highly effective at counteracting jet-lag, helping people adjust to different time zones. Insomnia can become a terrible burden when a habit of waking up in the middle of the night or finding it hard to get to sleep in the first place becomes entrenched. But regular meditation can help overcome disrupted sleeping patterns.

The relationship between meditation and sleep is an intriguing one in the Tibetan Buddhist tradition. Advanced meditators are known to be able to get by on very little sleep at night, their meditative state seemingly able to replicate the benefits of sleep without the need to spend so much time doing it.

Going further, while most of us would consider a good night's sleep to be a six- to eight-hour period of wombat-like unconsciousness, meditation yogis can take charge of their own consciousness even when asleep, directing their dreams to more subtle states of consciousness and insight than possible during the wakened state, a process known in the West as "lucid dreaming."[25] Stephen LaBerge, a lucid dreaming researcher, describes this in an intriguing way: "Waking experience is dream experience with physical constraints, while dream experience is waking experience without physical constraints."[26]

Meditation enhances mental clarity

Focusing our attention on just one thing over a sustained period of time goes against all our usual mental conditioning. For the vast majority of every minute our minds are rapidly switching from subject to subject, and/or our attention is divided between a number of different objects simultaneously—car radio, traffic lights, inner monologue about some worrying news. The movement and fragmentation of our attention is such second nature that focusing on just the one thing for any length of time is a serious challenge.

Even when our success is limited, and our mad monkey mind continues to make random excursions, the simple act of continuing to bring our attention back to the here and now marks a turning point. It's a form of mental discipline similar to what we may experience in study or training, but is even more singularly focused.

The mere act of applying this focus has an impact on our customary state of mental agitation. Even as complete newcomers to the practice, we find we have fewer intrusive thoughts during meditation. With practice, those distractions grow briefer in duration and further between. We begin to experience space between the distractions, periods when we can retain a relaxed focus on the object of meditation without gross agitation (see Chapter 3) of any kind.

A useful analogy is a glass of water you've scooped out of a gutter after a heavy downpour. Initially, the storm water is agitated, murky, a swirl of fragmented leaves, dirt, and assorted debris. It's so cloudy you couldn't possibly see anything through it. But leave that glass on a flat surface for half an hour and you know what happens. The agitation stops. The sediment settles. Pick up that glass and the water is clear enough for you to see right through.

When we meditate regularly and allow our usual mental agitation to settle, we achieve greater clarity. The contours of our world become more sharply distinct. Free from the swirling mental detritus that usually clouds our perception, we can see people, situations, and opportunities with fresh definition.

Mental clarity, the ability to see the wood for the trees, isn't something that can be measured objectively, but it's one of the defining experiences of all meditators. It's also one of the benefits of the practice most valued in an organizational context, mental clarity being one of the hallmarks of an effective leader.

My personal experience of this benefit came just a few months after I began meditating. I'd been a writer since boyhood, and from the age of eighteen until my early thirties I wrote many books in repeated, unsuccessful attempts to land that first, elusive publishing contract. My efforts included ten complete novels, all rejected by agents and publishers wherever I tried.

I began meditating simply to manage stress, without any idea that this strange new practice would impact on the ambition so close to my heart. But the subjective effect was like seeing the obvious for the first time. It was as though clouds I hadn't even realized were there parted and I caught sight of an opportunity quite clearly.

At the time I was living in London, where Tony Blair had just become prime minister. The media was full of stories of "spin doctors," portrayed as shadowy characters with unseen influence who lurked offstage. As it happened, I worked in public relations and felt well placed to comment on the phenomenon. Writing a short outline and just the first couple of chapters, I sent my book proposal to a handful of London publishers, and within a few weeks was made my first offer.

Of course I can't prove that I wouldn't have put two and two together had I not begun meditating, but it's an interesting coincidence—the kind that other meditators report and that I have continued to experience since then. For my own part, I have no doubt that improved mental clarity has helped me in very practical, worldly ways.

Related to my experience of that first accepted book proposal was another benefit of mindfulness: emotional regulation.

····· Meditation enhances emotional resilience ·····

When we're stressed out and our amygdala takes over from the executive function of our brain, we're more likely to do all kinds of things we wouldn't otherwise do. These include being short with people or lashing out in anger, responding emotionally instead of rationally to situations, becoming flustered and unable to make decisions, or making the wrong decisions.

While none of this is good for any of us, it's particularly dangerous for people whose lives quite literally depend on managing the most stressful situations on earth—soldiers.

It may also be hardly surprising that post-traumatic stress disorder is so prevalent among ex-military personnel. So it's more than interesting that in a collaboration between Georgetown University and the Mind Fitness Training Institute ("push-ups for the brain" anyone?) a study of US Marines who were given mindfulness training showed that "more time spent engaging in practice corresponded with greater self-reported mindfulness; increases in mindfulness were associated with decreases in perceived stress."[27]

If mindfulness has been shown to benefit soldiers operating in a war zone, what needs to be said about the benefits we could all experience in our lives and work?

Enhanced emotional regulation in the workplace is among the reasons why mindfulness is being embraced with such enthusiasm by organizations. Most of us are aware that issues caused by human interactions and "difficult" personalities are generally far harder to deal with than technical problems. When we're all less reactive and better able to get along with each other, workplaces are happier and more efficient all round.

We know from personal experience that the same thing can happen to us on two separate occasions and we'll react in two different ways. The difference usually has to do with our state of mind. When we're feeling spacious and at ease, we're far less likely to experience hostility, lash out, or press the "send" button on that blistering email.

Meditation not only supports greater equanimity and improved emotional resilience in the short term. Over the long term we get a lot better at dealing with the inevitable ups and downs in life. We come to realize that what seems like a problem now may be less so when we know the bigger picture.

The Zen story of the farmer who acquires a horse is a great illustration of this. In ancient Japan, where horses were regarded as a store of wealth, when the farmer bought his first horse, the local villagers came to see him, all excited. "How proud you must be to have a horse!" they congratulated him, to which he replied simply, "We'll see."

Soon afterwards the horse escaped and ran into the country. In no time at all the villagers were visiting, commiserating with the farmer. "What a tragic loss! How will you recover from this?" they wailed. Again, he replied simply, "We'll see."

The horse returned from the countryside—accompanied by two wild horses. They trotted into the paddock of their own volition—all the farmer had to do was close the gate. The villagers were beside themselves. "What an astonishing turnaround! From no horses now you have three!"

"We'll see."

Next, the farmer's son tried to break in one of the wild horses but was thrown off, breaking his leg. Just before harvest, the loss to the farmer of his main worker was a blow. There were more commiserations from the villagers. Another "We'll see."

Recruiters from the Imperial Army paid a visit to the village to round up all able-bodied young men for battle. Because the farmer's son had a broken leg, he was spared.

"We'll see."

Regular meditation improves our emotional resilience. Instead of being blown about by every piece of news like a piece of tissue paper, over time our minds become calmer and more stable. We become less up and down and more "We'll see."

Meditation increases self-compassion

Many of us direct our most judgemental attitudes and harshest language towards ourselves. It's a weird but all too common phenomenon. The sorts of fumbles, lapses of judgement, and mishaps we find easy to overlook if committed by friends or even acquaintances are intolerable if we commit them ourselves. We tell ourselves we've been utter fools, either silently or perhaps aloud in a torrent of expletive-laden vitriol. If we already suffer from poor self-esteem, every time we get something wrong serves only as further confirmation of our own existential uselessness. We may continually affirm our own self-image problems about, say, our appearance, abilities, self-discipline and performance—or inadequacies thereof—with an inner narrative of such unyielding cruelty that it would be considered abuse if directed at anyone else. With self-conditioning like this, is it any surprise that we may find it hard to abide in states of contentment and well-being?

Dr. Kristin Neff, an associate professor in human development and culture at the University of Texas, has made a study of self-compassion and the very urgent need for more of it.[28] She also notes the important role that mindfulness has to play in countering negative thoughts and feelings about the self and promoting self-compassion. According to Neff, self-compassion requires three interrelated elements. One is to see what happens to ourselves as part of the broader human experience rather than something that's specifically all about us. Another is to understand the simple need to extend the same kindness and understanding towards ourselves as we would to others when experiencing pain or failure, instead of being stridently self-critical. Importantly, the third element is mindfulness, which enables us to experience negativity without personally and strongly identifying with it. According to mindfulness teacher Michael Chaskalson:

Self-compassion protects you against the negative consequences of self-judgement, isolation, and depressive rumination. Because of its non-evaluative and interconnected nature, self-compassion counters the tendencies towards narcissism, self-centeredness, and downward social comparison . . .[29]

Buddhism has long understood the value of meditation in helping resolve our over-identification with the self, and the negative ways this can manifest itself, such as in arrogance—believing ourselves to be superior to others—or its opposite: poor self-esteem. Both arrogance and low self-esteem arise from too great a preoccupation with oneself, although this preoccupation plays out in opposite ways.

When we meditate, we recognize that this self with which we are all so preoccupied is nothing more than an idea we have at a particular moment—which will almost certainly be quite different from the idea we have at a different point in time. As we become more practiced at watching thoughts arise, abide and pass from our mind, we experience first hand the truth that all the thoughts we ever have, including thoughts of self, are transient. There's no concrete, permanent reality to get hung up about. Little by little we learn to let go, step freely and resist engaging in the fiction of loathsome or wonderful "me."

Meditation helps break tough habits

Many people struggle with breaking habits such as overeating, smoking, or substance abuse. A survey of 1,328 psychologists conducted by Consumer Reports and the American Psychological Association showed that seven out of ten psychologists considered mindfulness training an "excellent" or "good" strategy to assist in weight loss.[30]

Psychologists know that emotional factors are a critical reason people put on weight—and why they can struggle to lose it. Because so much of our emotional state arises directly from thoughts, better thought management helps us rein in unhappy feelings. When mindfulness is coupled with cognitive therapy it's especially powerful. Someone who has struggled with weight loss for years may come to hold beliefs such as "I don't have the willpower to lose weight" or "No matter what I do, I'll always be overweight." Any lapse in maintaining a weight-loss program—for example, eating two slices of pizza at a party instead of sticking to the salads—simply reinforces these beliefs. What other people may regard as a temporary lapse is viewed by this person as a major failure, and they could decide that, having blown the program, they might just as well finish the whole pizza . . . before moving on to the ice cream.

Some level of mindfulness enables us to see thoughts as just thoughts that come and go—not concrete facts or truths. We're less in the thrall of our thoughts. Their emotional impact is diminished. We're better able to live in the here and now rather than being engrossed in the harsh, negative, and untrue dramatization of a failed notional self.

This principle goes beyond unwanted eating habits. A University of Washington study of prisoners who were taught Vipassana meditation found that those who learned to meditate were significantly lower users of alcohol, marijuana, and crack cocaine after release than the treatment-as-usual controls. They also displayed far fewer psychiatric problems and more positive "psychosocial outcomes."[31]

Meditation makes music sound better

"The moment one gives close attention to anything, even a blade of grass, it becomes a mysterious, awesome, indescribably magnificent world in itself." Henry Miller's observation is now underpinned by interesting research evidence from Duke University's Center for Mindfulness Research and the University of Oregon's School of Music. In a recent study, the results of which were published in *Psychology of Music*, 132 participants were divided into groups, including some who engaged in mindfulness preparation before listening to music and control groups who did not.[32]

Mindfulness "significantly increased the participants' aesthetic and flow experience. Some were intense. They were really in the zone," according to Frank Diaz, a researcher who explored how mindfulness can enhance music engagement and performance.

Diaz points out that even if someone has listened to, or performed, a piece of music so many times they no longer get any pleasure out of it, their attention can be modified. Mindfulness "tends to take habituated responses and renews them. It's almost like a reset button."

It doesn't seem too much of a leap to suggest that the same holds true of any sensory experience. If music is more absorbing than otherwise, then maybe that blade of grass really is more indescribably magnificent, that aroma more vividly engaging, and that caramel-filled chocolate more delectably wonderful!

The way the world appears to us—out there versus in here—is, of course, a subject with life-changing implications that we'll explore in Chapter 9. For the moment, it's enough to know that mindfulness training can help us re-experience lives that may feel boringly humdrum with fresh clarity and wonder.

Meditation improves our working memory and academic performance

If we recollect the definition of mindfulness—paying attention to the present moment deliberately and non-judgementally—it should come as no surprise that training in it makes us better at paying attention. And when we pay attention to what's happening, we're more likely to remember it later.

Psychological researcher Michael Mrazek of the University of California, Santa Barbara, delivered emphatic evidence of just this when he randomly assigned 48 students to a mindfulness class or nutrition class. Classes met for 45 minutes four times a week over two weeks before students sat their Graduate Record Examinations (GREs).

The results were strikingly clear. Students who'd received mindfulness training showed an improved working memory capacity and accuracy on the GRE compared to those who'd been trained in nutrition. The reduced mind-wandering resulted in an average 16 percent higher GRE grade.[33]

If complete novices achieved this result after only eight sessions, what happens to our capabilities if we meditate every day for months or even years? Is it any surprise that more and more schools, colleges, companies, and others are encouraging people to practice mindfulness? Talk about a low-cost way to turbocharge productivity! And how long before we see the emergence of a Meditators" Union to demand higher pay for those with superior attention spans?

···· Meditation rewires the brain for happiness ····

Dr. Richard Davidson, director of the Laboratory for Affective Neuroscience at the University of Wisconsin, has played a pioneering role in using fMRI (functional magnetic resonance imaging) equipment to monitor real-time changes to brain activity during meditation.

The use of fMRI has shown that when people are emotionally distressed—anxious, angry, depressed—the brain's circuits in the right prefrontal cortex are the most active. By way of contrast, when people are happy, energized, or upbeat, activity shifts to the left prefrontal cortex. Having monitored brain activity in hundreds of students, Dr. Davidson found that we all have a "set point" for happiness. No matter what happens to us—losing a loved one in a car accident or winning the lottery—after a while we revert to our set point. Whether this set point is towards the grumpy right side of the prefrontal cortex or the happier left side varies from person to person.[34]

But significantly, that set point can be shifted. Dr. Davidson collaborated with Dr. Jon Kabat-Zinn, founder of the Mindfulness-Based Stress Reduction Clinic at the University of Massachusetts Medical School. In a study involving corporate employees, to whom Dr. Kabat-Zinn taught mindfulness methods for about three hours over a two-month period, fMRI scanning revealed a shift from the negative, right side of the spectrum towards the left. Employees themselves reported feeling more energized, less anxious, and more purposeful about their work.

Even in a relatively short period of time, inexperienced meditators can begin to alter their overall mood state. So what happens if we keep on meditating? Dr. Davidson had the good fortune to meet a highly experienced meditator, a senior Tibetan lama, who agreed to undergo the fMRI process. It should come as no surprise that of the 175 people Dr. Davidson had tested until that time, the lama was positioned on the most extreme left-hand side of the happiness spectrum.

Subsequent work carried out at the W.M. Keck Laboratory for Functional Brain Imaging and Behavior involved wiring up volunteers to an electroencephalograph (EEG), a net of 256 electrical sensors, while they meditated. Ten student volunteers with no meditation training were used as a control group whose readings were to be compared with those of eight highly advanced practitioners who were Tibetan monks.

The results of the study were dramatic. While the control group showed a slight increase in gamma-wave activity when they were asked to meditate, readings from the monks showed much greater activation of fast-moving and unusually powerful gamma waves. What's more, wave movement through their brains was far more efficiently organized. Those monks who had spent the most years meditating had the highest levels of gamma waves, some of them producing wave activity more powerful than had ever been recorded previously.

This "dose response," reported in the *Washington Post*, helps establish a clear case of cause and effect. In simple terms, the more we meditate, the better we get at it and the happier we feel. Neuroplasticity helps account for this. Although scientists previously believed that the connections between brain cells were fixed once we reached adulthood, they now know this to be untrue. The brain continues to evolve and opens up new neural pathways, physically reshaping our brains—a subject explored in vivid detail by psychiatrist Norman Doidge in *The Brain that Changes Itself.*[35]

Meditation changes our brains. It shifts our default mood "set point" to the left. In short, it rewires us for happiness. To quote Dr. Davidson, "What we have found is that the trained mind, or brain, is physically different from the untrained one."[36]

In essence

This chapter summarizes only some of the benefits of meditation, but enough, I hope, to provide a level of understanding about the basic mechanics of the practice from current scientific and therapeutic perspectives. These help reveal not only why meditation helps us deal with mental and physical challenges—in essence moving us from dysfunctional to functional—but also how meditation can empower us to move from functional to super-functional. From zero to plus ten. To be the best we can be.

If we were to review these benefits collectively, how might we describe them? Four overall qualities of meditation that come to mind are that it is:

1 *holistic.* Even though most people come to the practice for one specific reason, such as help in managing stress, pain,

or high blood pressure, we quickly discover that the impact of mindfulness is systemic, delivering benefits well beyond what we originally signed up for. Writing in *The Healing Power of Meditation*, Dr. Jon Kabat-Zinn says:

Often transformation happens across a much wider range of domains than the person was expecting or even felt was possible. Sometimes it is a larger understanding of who one is—beyond the stories, the personal narratives, the attachment to the personal pronouns.[37]

Mindfulness practice takes us well beyond specific symptoms and even their causes. Little by little it begins to transform our whole sense of who and what we are.

2 *powerful*. Sitting still for ten to twenty minutes a day and focusing on your breath may seem suspiciously simple. How could all the amazing benefits described above flow from that? But as we've seen, in neuroscientific or cognitive terms the changes are profound. These shifts have extraordinary impacts on both mind and body.

We're so used in the West to turning to outer, material fixes for things, it seems we've been culturally conditioned to overlook solutions using more subtle, inner dynamics. Only now are we starting to awaken to this complementary approach and appreciate its extraordinary effectiveness.

3 *enduring*. In just the same way that regular physical exercise has benefits going way beyond the subjective experience of any single session, so too does meditation. Its impacts endure well after we've stood up from the cushion, effecting a gradual but increasing shift in the way we experience reality. So disproportionate is this impact that the short time we may spend meditating each morning seems a small price to pay for our enhanced abilities to think, feel, and act for the twenty-three hours and however many minutes of the day we're *not* meditating.

4 *self-reinforcing*. The more we do it, the better we get at it, and the greater the change. As Aristotle famously put it, "We are what we repeatedly do." By practicing meditation we become more mindful—calmer, happier, more fulfilled, and aware.

And all this is only the beginning.

5

How mindfulness benefits organizations

Most of us aren't employed for our good looks. We're employed for our minds. But how many of us consciously seek out ways to optimize our most important asset?

CLARE GOODMAN, ORGANIZATIONAL MINDFULNESS

The overwhelming focus of mindfulness research to date has been its benefits to individuals. But what about organizations? Mindfulness programs are increasingly being introduced by companies as large and diverse as Google, General Mills, LinkedIn, Twitter, Barclays, KPMG, Carlsberg, Sony, and General Electric, to name but a few. At the outset of this chapter I should declare an interest: along with my business partner Clare Goodman, I manage Organizational Mindfulness, or OM, a company that delivers mindful leadership programs to a range of public- and private-sector organizations. Clare and I have experienced, first-hand, the many interrelated improvements that occur when groups of company staff attend mindfulness sessions together.

What is it about the practice of mindfulness that's winning the support of hard-headed corporate leaders? And why are they encouraging employees to spend productive work time engaged in meditation—an activity that appears to deliver no immediate bottom-line benefit?

Perhaps the best way to begin answering these questions is to look at how we deal with stress—only this time from an organizational perspective.

The stress pandemic

"Going to work" and "experiencing stress" are interchangeable terms for most of us. While this is not inherently a bad thing—like elastic bands we all require some level of stress to realize our potential—maintaining the *right* level of stress is at best an ongoing challenge and at worst may feel like a hopelessly impossible task.

Never before have so many people worked such long hours to meet such daunting productivity targets. Never has the environment in which we operate been so complex and interconnected that, say, the factional hostilities of political groups in the Middle East can put global stock markets on edge and bring horror relentlessly into our homes. Never have so many of us been so instantly contactable and increasingly expected to relinquish our "out of hours" personal time to deal with work-related messages and emails. Whether it's taking calls on the mobile while walking along busy lunch-hour sidewalks, sitting in bed with the laptop, replying to work emails at 10 p.m., or spending precious weekend hours working on documents that just can't be written in a frenetic, demanding workplace where our attention is constantly subjected to numberless demands, the end result is the same. We're all caught up in a stress pandemic propelled by a number of imperatives that show no sign of abating. These include:

- technological advancements demanding immediate, round-the-clock responsiveness
- unprecedented volatility in external operating environments
- increasingly onerous regulatory requirements
- greater complexity in managing disparate stakeholder groups
- tougher performance measurements
- constant need for change
- ongoing demands to do more with fewer resources.

While these imperatives provide the overall context for workplace stress, depending on where you are within an organization, you may experience pressures in different ways. In *Seeing Systems*,[1] Barry Oshry, a leadership development specialist, describes the following broad categories of personnel. Most of us who've worked in organizations will have little difficulty recognizing their dynamics:

1 *Top*. You have overall responsibility for a significant part of your work or organization. You're burdened by what feels like unmanageable complexity, caught up in destructive turf wars, fighting fires when you should be shaping the system's future.

2 *Middle*. You're caught between the conflicting demands and priorities coming from Tops and Bottoms, alienated from them, non-cooperative and competitive when you should be working together to coordinate system processes.

3 *Bottom*. You're mainly subject to initiatives over which you have no control, oppressed by what you see as distant and uncaring Tops, trapped by stifling pressures to conform. Your negative feelings towards Tops and Middles distract you from putting your creative energies into the delivery of products and services.

Dysfunctional response to stress number 1: multitasking

We all respond to stress in our own particular ways, but in the workplace there are several common, dysfunctional reactions.

Multi-tasking is perhaps the most obvious of these. It's still hailed as a positive attribute by some, and as leadership experts Richard Boyatzis and Annie McKee explain:

People who are good at doing several complex tasks at once . . . are often valued in our organizations . . . Leaders need to stay focused and efficient for months, sometimes years, on end. They have to keep lots of big ideas at the top of their mind, concurrently, including a huge amount of detail and information about their increasingly complex environment. Many executives feel that mega-multitasking becomes a badge of honor.[2]

The truth, however, is that multi-tasking makes people less productive, less effective, and is ultimately unsustainable. The implications for this on organizations are both wide-ranging and profound. Media multitasking in particular has a deleterious effect on concentration and productivity. The implicit expectation for executives to work on complex spreadsheets at the same time as monitoring inboxes, taking calls on the landline and mobile, dealing with colleagues who have myriad "Can you just . . ." requests, and quite possibly attending to online updates can only have one possible outcome: cognitive overload. This in turn results in poorer overall performance. When we're concentrating on a complex task and we're interrupted, it can take a long time to resume our focus. Repeated interruptions inevitably mean the overall quality of our output is diminished.

Because our brains are serial processors, media multitasking specifically makes us less productive, less responsive, and less nimble. The increased agitation of our mind doesn't just slow us down. Little by little it degrades our ability to concentrate, in the present moment, in depth and in detail, on any one thing for any length of time. A Stanford University study from 2009 provided definitive evidence that heavy media multitaskers were slower in their ability to switch to new activities, were more easily distracted by irrelevant details, and had poorer memory recall than lighter media multitaskers.[3]

When we multitask we're more likely to experience our "attention blink," suffering from gaps in concentration. We're also less effective in our interactions with others. We may be looking but we don't see the expressions in others" faces, we may listen but we don't hear their tone of voice. We miss out on potentially vital cues we should be paying attention to.

In an interview with National Public Radio, Stanford Psychology Department's Professor Clifford Nass observed with droll humor: "The research is almost unanimous, which is very rare in social science, and it says that people who chronically multitask show an enormous range of deficits. They're basically terrible at all sorts of cognitive tasks, including multitasking."[4]

Trying to get on top of our workload by doing a number of things at once is not only ineffective, it also degrades our ability to concentrate in the future. Neither of these is desirable on an individual level, and both have negative consequences for the organizations where people work.

Dysfunctional response to stress number 2: tunnel vision

The opposite response to multitasking is being goal-focused: fixing our sights on the objective, the strategy, the challenge we face, and heading towards it to the exclusion of all else.

Like multitasking, being goal-driven is often held to be a positive. Being clear about what's needed and going all out to get it may seem admirable and disciplined, but it has a shadow side in the form of tunnel vision. As Boyatzis and McKee explain:

> When focusing too narrowly, people have little tolerance (or mental space) for unrelated thoughts. We ignore extraneous data, including internal thoughts and feelings and external

information. The result, of course, is that we miss a great
deal. We may not see subtle patterns, may not pay attention
to the anomalies that can point us in a new direction or give
early warning about problems. In essence, we can develop
tunnel vision—seeing only what we need to see to reach the
goal. This, of course, means we miss information that tells
us that the goal (or the target, or the strategy) might need
to change.[5]

Tunnel vision is what happens when we train our minds *not* to notice what's going on. Far from paying attention to the present moment, deliberately and non-judgementally, we're paying attention to whatever it is we want to achieve and screening out anything we regard as superfluous to that objective. The trouble is, in striving for a particular objective, we'll try to solve problems based on our past experience, not on what's happening here and now. We're also less likely to be capable of the broad thinking and creativity that fuel innovation—which is more necessary than ever to gain a competitive advantage.

Most of us who've worked in organizations recognize the traits of the executive who's so wrapped up in their own activities they pay little attention to what anyone else has to say; have little capacity or time for empathy; are intolerant of suggestions, much less constructive criticism; and show no appreciation for innovative ideas unless they advance their own narrowly cast agenda.

In the end, the executive may deliver on a particular set of outcomes, but at what cost, and how relevant will those outcomes still be?

Dysfunctional response to stress number 3: burnout

Burnout is a state of emotional, mental, and physical exhaustion caused by excessive and prolonged stress. When staff are burned out they lack enthusiasm and motivation; are frustrated, despairing, and cynical about their workplace; feel unappreciated; and have the sense that every day is a bad day.

Research suggests that those at greatest risk of burnout are those who have high levels of motivation and commitment to the work they do, and for whom it's important to find meaning in their work. When this motivation meets with what they perceive as constant obstacles, complexity, demands to do irrelevant compliance-driven tasks, or interpersonal conflict, the result is despair.

When employees suffer from burnout they have less empathy towards colleagues or clients, take more time off work and have frequent thoughts about resigning. The burned-out colleague may come back from vacations feeling recharged and reinvigorated, but a return to burnout is inevitable unless the dynamics of their position have changed . . . or unless they develop a new capacity to manage stress.

The impact of workplace stress on an organization

- Increased absenteeism
- Increased staff turnover
- Reduced productivity
- Reduced employee engagement
- Greater interpersonal conflict
- Reduced job satisfaction
- Poor teamwork—"them and us" attitudes
- Reduced will and ability to solve problems
- Reduced ability to handle change
- Executive performance compromised by multitasking and/or tunnel vision
- Reduced innovation and creativity
- Breakdown of trust
- Decreased discretionary effort
- Cynicism, low morale, and burnout

The benefits of mindfulness
in the workplace

Workplace stress frequently starts at the top of an organization and cascades down, creating a variety of negative impacts. Some of the problem areas listed above are so much a part of the corporate landscape that we become habituated to them, believing them to be unavoidable if regrettable elements of working life. Even if we moved to another organization, would it be any different?

Many workplaces mistake busy-ness for productivity, attendance for getting the job done. Being busy becomes like a status symbol, with the busiest people rewarded for their busy-ness and the culture of busy-ness perpetuated. Some people seem to thrive on a high-adrenalin state, and in seeking to perpetuate it they draw others into their vortex.

The good news is that a growing body of research shows how the practice of mindfulness can both help eliminate stress-induced dysfunctionality and cultivate more positive values, delivering beneficial and often quite unexpected impacts. As more and more companies implement mindfulness programs in the workplace, they're discovering the multiple benefits of this extraordinary but gentle practice.

Just as, on a personal basis, the benefits of mindfulness are holistic, going beyond whatever immediate goal we may have sought to achieve, similarly organizations are discovering that mindfulness programs can be catalysts for positive change across multiple disciplines, dynamics, and teams. We can point to some impressive performance indicators revealed by early studies. And there are other areas, less easily measured, where organizations are discovering in mindfulness programs an unexpectedly powerful new resource.

Mindfulness leads to improved attendance rates

Employees taking sick or personal days cost organizations a fortune in the form of lower productivity. To be specific, that's roughly $3,125 per year per absent employee acccording to one analysis.[6] The average absenteeism level is seven days a year in the United Kingdom but ten days in the US—and as a general rule, higher absenteeism reflects a sick organizational culture.

Implementing mindfulness programs has been shown to improve attendance rates dramatically. One study among workers at Transport for London showed that health-related absenteeism fell by 50 percent after participation in a mindfulness program. More specifically, time taken off for stress, depression, and anxiety fell by 70 percent in the three years following the course. Employees who attended the course pointed to a number of improvements in their quality of life: 79 percent said they were more able to relax, 53 percent had greater job satisfaction, and 80 percent reported happier relationships.[7]

People who find satisfaction and purpose in their jobs are less likely to quit than those who don't. According to research by the US-based iOpener Institute, in a company with 1,000 employees, increased levels of happiness in the workplace reduce the cost of employee turnover by 46 percent. iOpener provides similarly impressive metrics for the reduced cost of sick leave (19 percent) and increased performance and productivity (12 percent).[8]

If the prospect of particular deadlines, workloads, or other challenges makes us feel productive and fulfilled without being unduly stressed, we're far likelier to enjoy the experience and feel greater job satisfaction. This is one of the key premises of mindfulness at work. Even if the demands of the job don't change, our attitude towards them can—and this shift can enable us to experience our working reality in a very different way.

In *The Mindful Workplace*, UK-based mindfulness teacher Michael Chaskalson describes how people who are more mindful have negative thoughts less frequently, and when they do they are better able to let them go. They also have a more stable sense of self-esteem that's less contingent on external factors. With a greater awareness and acceptance of their emotions, they recover more quickly from bad moods.[9]

Regular meditators also enjoy enhanced attention, job performance, productivity, and better relationships with colleagues—all of which reduce workplace stress. And as we saw in the last chapter, mindfulness also improves our memory and the quality of our work. Meditation increases our ability to concentrate and maintain our attention—which is of particular value in noisy or stressful environments. Meditators are also better at learning and retaining information, as well as handling novelty and change.

Researchers from West Virginia University carried out a study of 141 employees, 44 percent of whom reported a constant state of stress before completing a mindfulness program. After the program, participants reported a 30 percent decrease in both psychological distress and medical symptoms, as well as significant improvements according to a battery of twenty-one different markers. Two years later, 92 percent of participants were still meditating regularly.

A separate study at General Mills showed that after a seven-week mindfulness course, 83 percent of participants said they were "taking time each day to optimize my personal productivity"—a dramatic rise from the 23 percent who agreed with this statement before the course. Eighty-two percent said they now made time to eliminate tasks with limited productivity value—an increase from 32 percent.

The response of senior executives was particularly striking: 80 percent said they'd experienced a positive change in their ability to make better decisions, while 89 percent said they'd become better listeners.[10]

.... *Mindfulness leads to better teamwork* ....

Because of the correlation between mindfulness and emotional intelligence, people who are mindful are better able to override or alter their interpretations of situations and resist acting on impulse. They also have higher levels of self-awareness. Together, these result in better social skills and ability to cooperate, and improved teamwork. Instead of reacting in habitual ways, perhaps lashing out under pressure or automatically slipping into passive-aggressive mode, staff at all levels enjoy more mental space, clarity, and calm, enabling them to respond to perceived challenges in a more productive, supportive, and cohesive way.

Boyatzis and McKee use the term "resonant leadership" to describe how effective leaders can attune to people and amplify what's best in them. This same principle applies to teams. A resonant team is one whose members are attuned to each other, whereas a dissonant team is inharmonious.

When a group of staff meets regularly to meditate, even if only once or twice a month for twenty minutes, they're drawn together by an intangible but powerful bond. Participation in a process where everyone is on the same level, which carries no burden of expectation and where, in a relaxed and open state, observations may be safely shared, has effects quite beyond what appearances may suggest. Clare Goodman and I have had the privilege of leading mindfulness programs in organizations over a sustained period of time, and the benefit on team dynamics has become so self-evident that we've coined the phrase "A company that sits together, knits together." It's a wonderful thing to be a part of!

Mindfulness leads to enhanced interpersonal relations

People who are mindful have improved levels of empathy, making them better able to see things from another person's point of view. They're better at communicating, and because they're less emotionally invested in a particular perspective, are less likely to think negatively about colleagues, even when they disagree with them on some issues. They're also less likely to respond defensively or aggressively when they feel threatened. This significantly reduces the likelihood of interpersonal conflict.

Mindfulness programs can have a significant impact in cases where such conflicts already exist. Relationships shift into a different gear when we become willing to see others as human beings with their own worries and concerns and hopes for happiness rather than difficult individuals who are out to cause us trouble. While delivering programs into workplaces, I've seen intractably hostile relationships morph into quietly supportive ones without a word being said—both parties allowing bygones to be bygones and moving into the more positive territory enabled by a calmer, more panoramic, and empathetic perspective.

Resolutions of this kind are not only heart-warming on a personal level, they also have an organizational pay-off when individuals and teams are more willing to pull together to achieve collective goals.

Mindfulness leads to greater creativity and innovation

It's no coincidence that some of the most successful companies in the world, operating in the most ferociously competitive consumer markets, are among the most enthusiastic advocates of mindfulness. Each year Google hosts the Wisdom Conference, where business leaders, mindfulness coaches, and meditation gurus congregate, including executives from the likes of Yahoo, Cisco Systems, Twitter, LinkedIn, and Facebook. What these organizations have in common is an understanding of the value of mindfulness as a means of unleashing creativity. And in the words of Professor Michael Porter, "innovation is the central issue in economic prosperity."[11]

The optimization of business products and services is the central focus of most businesses. It's increasingly recognized that the area with by far the greatest potential for optimization is the imagination and creativity of an organization's own staff. It's well-nigh impossible to come up with innovative ideas when you're trapped in a cycle of mindless, habitual behavior. Ditto when you're feeling stressed out, anxious, or fearful. Hence the implementation by Google of "innovation time off," where staff can do whatever they like every Friday as long as they stay in the office—a policy responsible for half of all new product launches.

The regular practice of meditation represents a multi-faceted aid to creativity. Writing in *The Huffington Post*, lawyer and creativity consultant Flynn Coleman says:

> mindfulness is at the core of all creative activity . . . When
> we embrace the present, the stress of our past and our future

fades, and we can expand the boundaries of our imagination. Once we strip away the calcified assumptions about ourselves and our world, we can see everything from a fresh perspective. It's here, as Thoreau wrote, that we discover new ideas "like falling meteors," suddenly appearing before us "with a flash and an explosion."[12]

When we practice mindfulness we let go of assumptions, which enables us to see familiar challenges through fresh eyes. We have greater clarity and objectivity—which allows us to see solutions that may be staring us in the face, only we were too distracted to recognize them. Calm and relaxed, we're also more playful, and it's on this rising tide of vitality, openness, and joie de vivre that creativity is born.

In neuroscientific parlance, as we saw in Chapter 4, meditators have been shown to produce much higher levels of gamma-wave signals than non-meditators. Gamma-waves typically appear when the brain draws together a number of disparate attributes, creating "aha" moments.

As a writer, I can point to two specific instances when meditation has led directly to important creative break-throughs. In the last chapter I explained how the clarity of my newfound meditation practice helped me identify a way to apply my enthusiasm for writing to a subject that would be of interest to publishers. You could say that I saw a connection, joined the dots, and was able to bring together a product and a market at just the right time.

The second instance was when I came up with the idea for *The Dalai Lama's Cat*. I can still remember, quite vividly, arising from a Saturday-morning meditation with a powerful narrative voice in my head, one so compelling I sat down and wrote the first few pages of the book immediately. The idea of the Dalai Lama having a cat who "wrote" a book was one I'd been toying with, on and off, for some months, but I'd yet to discover the voice of the narrator, which was critical to finding an entry point to the story. Then, like Thoreau's flash and explosion, it just happened. There was no need for analysis, scenario-setting, or strategic mapping. In a calm, relaxed, and meditative state, a solution arose quite effortlessly in my mind, coherent and fully resolved.

While many of the whys and wherefores of creativity remain a mystery, creating the conditions in which innovation can flourish is less so. Relaxing into a state where our minds are benevolent and open to the field of all possibilities, we're very much more likely to experience an "aha" moment.

Mindfulness leads to better leadership

Annie McKee and colleagues identify three myths about corporate leadership in *Becoming a Resonant Leader*.[13] The first is that "smart is good enough." While no one disputes the importance of business savvy and highly developed intellectual skills when leading complex organizations, intelligence alone doesn't cut it. The overwhelming weight of recent research shows that emotional and social intelligence are far more effective predictors of leadership effectiveness. There's a saying that people don't leave their jobs . . . they leave their bosses. A leader who can't retain and motivate strong team members is destined to lose them to the competition.

Myth number two is that "mood doesn't matter." In the stretch to hit business targets, whatever they may be, the notion that as long as you get there the psychological state of colleagues is secondary is also a fallacy. If the cost to an organization is chronic stress, suspicion, cynicism, and burnout, whatever is achieved will be a hollow victory, and one less likely to be repeated. Instead, a team that enjoys higher levels of satisfaction, teamwork, creativity, and optimism sets the organization on a far more sustainable trajectory.

The third myth is that "great leaders can thrive on constant pressure." The truth is that no matter how alpha a leader, they're only human. Without balance, leaders lose their edge, their effectiveness is diminished, and the consequences are bleak both for them and the organizations they lead.

It's significant that mindfulness practice holds the key in responding to all three of these myths. Improved mental clarity, emotional regulation, stress management, and ability to empathize—mindfulness benefits we've already looked at in some detail—are precisely what we need to develop emotional and social intelligence, enhance positive team dynamics, and deal with pressure.

In *The Mindful Leader*, mindfulness teacher Michael Carroll writes:

mindful leadership is tremendously practical because it rests on a simple yet profound insight that expands the entire notion of leadership altogether: *all human beings instinctively want to offer their best to others and in turn inspire others to do the same, and this can be done by anyone, anywhere, anytime* ... [original italics][14]

As leaders, if we wish to inspire our team to give of their best, we need to be attuned to them, aware of dynamics within interactions, meetings, and teams, and able to respond openly and authentically. If we seek to lead coherent, thriving organizations to sustainable success, among the qualities that will serve us best are those optimized by the practice of mindfulness.

To what extent is it the business of an organization to foster a sense of meaning and purpose among its staff in the work they do? Is a fair day's wage for a fair day's work not reward enough?

Given the sheer amount of time we spend at work, and the level of mental and emotional resources our jobs demand, the truth is that we require more than only money to motivate us. People on regular salaries soon habituate to their income level, so that even the excitingly large increase they may have enjoyed when moving to a new job quickly becomes the norm. Outgoings soon rise to adjust to income. Asked why we go to work, we may reflexively answer that the mortgage won't pay itself. But money and the improved lifestyle that more of it will bring don't adequately explain all of our behavior or even some of the most important elements of it.

Most people also seek some level of validation that their work is valued and important to others—and that they too are therefore valued and important. Some are driven by a burning wish to make their mark, whether that's as modest as a new form of reporting within an existing corporate structure or as entrepreneurial as developing a revolutionary new medical treatment. Others become passionate about causes, from the regulation of the financial services industry, to ending bear-bile farming in South-East Asia.

From an organizational perspective, what matters is that staff members are able to find in their work something of value and importance to them personally. Few things are more infectious than enthusiasm, however expressed, and a motivated, purposeful team will always seriously outgun competitors who lack the same drive.

Paradoxically, meaning in work isn't something organizations can transfer into employees' minds as easily as money into their bank accounts. It must be determined by the employees themselves.

One of my favorite stories involves a monk who taught meditation to long-term prisoners. After regular visits to the prison over the years, he was asked by one of the inmates to describe a typical day at the monastery. The regime he described was harsh: up at 5 a.m. for two hours of meditation, light breakfast, more meditation and teaching, followed by labor in the monastery gardens, a main meal at lunchtime comprising whatever food the monks could grow themselves or had been donated to them, more work in the afternoon, only soup for dinner, meditation in the evening, and an early night, and no TV, newspapers, internet access, alcohol, or conjugal visits *ever*. In comparison, life in the prison was leisurely and relatively indulgent. The inmates were so struck by the austerity of the monk's life that one of them spontaneously exclaimed: "If it all gets too much, you could always come and live with us here!"

The monk reflected afterwards how, for all its hardships, there was a long waiting list of monks who wanted to join the monastery. By contrast, if the prison doors were to be opened, within minutes not a single inmate would remain. In summary, it's not our circumstances that make us happy or unhappy, it's whether or not they're an authentic reflection of what matters to us.

Whether your organization is a monastery or a prison to its employees depends less on external conditions than on their hearts and minds. Are they able to find something of value in their work? Do their co-workers bring out the best in them? Are they able to find meaning in what they do beyond "another day, another dollar"?

While organizations can't provide these answers, they can provide the context within which people are most likely to discover them for themselves. In truth, most busy people don't spend much time contemplating the meaning of life, except perhaps after several glasses of wine late on a Sunday afternoon. Generally speaking, it's not an undertaking for which we're culturally trained. But the regular practice of meditation creates the space within which meaning is to be found. Not wishy-washy, pseudo-philosophical notions, but meaning that reflects the authentic nature of our minds.

While this subject is discussed in much more detail later in the book, to cut to the chase, what we discover is that our sense of fulfilment and purpose is most likely to be satisfied at the deepest level when we can use our abilities for the service of others or for a cause that's greater than ourselves. Meditation reveals not only that mind's true nature is lucid, clear, and boundless with potential, but also that the qualities of our own mind—even if caught only in glimpses through the agitation— are imbued with a natural altruism, integrity, and compassion. Meditation reconnects us to the wellspring of our own better nature. And when we reconnect regularly, we begin to reframe our experience of reality to accord with it. We willingly seek out opportunities to be of service to others. We value the truth that in giving happiness to those around us, we ourselves are the first beneficiaries.

The advantage of this to organizations is self-evident: a team of people motivated at the most profound level to be outward-focused, to resonate positively with their colleagues, and to deliver value. When employees find greater meaning in their work, organizational goals are more likely to be advanced. As some of the most successful companies in the world are currently showing us, the opportunities for organizations to impact society in extraordinary and profound ways, well beyond the commercial, are only now beginning to be realized.

The business case for mindfulness is multifaceted, powerful, and still very much a work in progress. The data we already have on metrics such as absenteeism, staff turnover, productivity, and employee engagement are evidence enough of the positive impact of mindfulness in the workplace. Less hard to quantify are the missed opportunities arising from poor teamwork, alienated co-workers, dysfunctional, stressed executives, cynical staff, and an organization that becomes so internally focused it loses sight of what's happening in the world around it.

Here, too, mindfulness offers a vital antidote. While difficult to quantify, the repeatable and observable experience of organizations that have implemented mindfulness and/or meditation programs demonstrates often dramatic improvements in interpersonal relations, teamwork, innovation, leadership, and that critical but seldom discussed motivator we all need to commit ourselves wholeheartedly to our work: a sense of meaning.

6

Ten tips for getting into the meditation habit

There is nothing whatsoever
That is not made easier through acquaintance

SHANTIDEVA

After you've been meditating a while, you'll almost certainly find yourself in a conversation that goes something like this:

"So, Mary tells me you meditate."

"That's right."

"I tried to meditate once."

"Really?"

"I tried to empty my mind and think of nothing, but I couldn't."

"Hmm."

"Didn't work."

"How long did you meditate for?"

"Fifteen minutes."

"No, I mean, how often?"

"Oh, a couple of times. I didn't have to do it again. You see, I have a mind that's just too active!" At this point they may regard you with a look of puzzlement. "I don't know how you manage it."

When you find yourself thus cornered, my advice is to change the subject or step away. To begin with, I've never come across an instruction from a credible teacher suggesting you should "empty your mind" or "think of nothing," but these are commonly held mistaken beliefs. Given that instructions for meditation are fairly simple, if your conversational bore got that wrong, what else did they misunderstand? As for possessing a uniquely overactive mind, nothing could be more delusional— we *all* think too much. That's the point! But perhaps the most absurd assumption, one that frankly borders on the insane, is that meditation could be subjectively judged as "working" or "not working" on the basis of a couple of sessions. Or even a couple of weeks of sessions.

The gym I go to had a sign up one January for all those New Year's resolutioners, saying something like: "6 weeks for you to notice. 8 weeks for close friends. 12 weeks for others." I wish that same sign could go up outside meditation studios and temples around the world.

Could you imagine someone saying they tried going to the gym a couple of times but "it didn't work" because after twenty minutes of lifting barbells their biceps failed to bulge pleasingly through their T-shirt, at which point they decided their body was so uniquely puny they would never respond to further effort?

Why should our minds be any different?

At the end of my "Introduction to Meditation" seminars I deliver several times each year, I'm often told by a number of people how inspired they are by the benefits, how much they enjoyed the practice, how eager they are to take things further. I don't believe these people are being insincere—I'm also quite sure they mean what they say at the time. But they return to their daily grind and, despite their good intentions, they don't follow through. When we hold follow-up mornings six weeks later, we usually see only 40 percent of the original group.

Knowing how to meditate and even having a strong initial motivation obviously isn't enough. Possessing the tools to cultivate the *habit* of meditation is also critically important.

Here are a few suggestions about how to do just that. I've gathered them from a variety of sources over the years. Some of them may seem immediately useful—or not. I suggest you read through them and choose those that suit your particular circumstances right now.

1. Don't procrastinate

This is probably the number-one reason why many people aren't meditating: they're putting it off until a mythical time when it will be easier to accommodate in their busy lives. They'll start meditating when the corporate takeover is completed, when they've finished their exams, when they've moved houses, when Jupiter aligns with Mars.

Procrastination may well arise from a positively intended wish to give meditation its best possible start—but this wish is deceptive. Whatever seems overwhelmingly important today will be replaced by an equally compelling focus of attention tomorrow.

Not having time to meditate is often used to justify procrastination, but let's get real. We're only talking about ten minutes—the equivalent of three or four TV commercial breaks. Most people watch hours of television every day. Are ten minutes really so hard to find?

When I began meditating, I set my alarm clock ten minutes earlier. It wasn't that difficult an adjustment. After a shave, shower, and shampoo, I sat for ten minutes and meditated—a routine unvaried twenty years later, except that the ten minutes has grown, quite naturally, to an hour.

"But the traffic outside/the kids/the television are a noisy distraction," is another reason given for waiting for a time when these factors can be controlled. Obviously, the more external distractions you can eliminate, the better. If that involves shutting yourself in the laundry room for peace and quiet, so be it.

I like the story told by Jetsunma Tenzin Palmo, an Englishwoman who went to India, became a nun, and meditated in a cave in the Himalayas for twelve years. It would be hard to think of a more extreme take on "getting away from it all." Could there be a more radical way to remove yourself from the bustle of city life to the tranquil isolation of the mountains? Once in her remote cave, however, Jetsunma discovered that she shared the mountains with a pack of wolves. And whether roaming past her cave or somewhat further away, they would sometimes howl incessantly.

Which leads to one inevitable conclusion: even if you were to find yourself in a cave in the Himalayas, chances are your circumstances would be no more free of distraction than you can make them right now![1]

2. Set yourself the six-week meditation challenge

Other people may benefit from meditation—but will you? You may be perfectly willing to accept the experience of scientists and sages, but what about your own experience? What's the best way for you to put meditation to the test?

I recommend you set yourself the six-week meditation challenge. This seems a reasonable period of time to give meditation a fair go and see if you can subjectively detect any change. You could try a one-month challenge, but if you go this route you'll have to be punctilious about not missing a day. I prefer six weeks because it allows a bit of leeway for the occasional lapse here and there.

The concept of four-week or six-week challenges has grown in popularity recently, whether it's to get fit, quit sugar, lose weight, or change breakfast cereal. It's a powerful idea because you feel you're making only a finite commitment.

That said, scientific studies show that repetition is the key to effecting lasting changes. The best way to create a positive habit is to repeatedly do something over a period of weeks, to make it so much a part of our routine that, like brushing our teeth, it's not something we decide whether or not we'll do today. We do it because that's what we always do before going to bed. Many people probably simply forget to meditate because they fail to establish a meditation routine. This is why creating some sort of environmental cue is important to remind us—at least in the early days.

Decide when you're going to slot meditation into your life, such as between getting dressed in the morning and having breakfast—and stick to it. According to psychologist Meredith Fuller, "We can actually lay new neuron pathways in our brains by repeating an action or way of thinking. The aim is to transform a new activity into an automatic habit. With repetition, it becomes something we do without thinking; in fact, we experience discomfort if we don't do it."[2]

Curiously, this was exactly how I first stumbled upon the benefits of meditation. After about five or six weeks of quite regular practice, I had one of those days when everything that could go wrong seemed to. I found myself getting angrier and angrier. It was only around lunchtime that I suddenly realized I hadn't meditated for a few days. Life had got in the way and I'd missed my morning sessions. In neuroscientific terms, my insula was now fully engaged with the analytical parts of my brain, creating a vicious downward spiral. Subjectively, I felt as though I had lost an invisible layer of protective clothing.

I later discovered that the legendary Buddhist sage Shantideva had once said we can't cover the whole world with leather to avoid stepping on thorns, but we can wear a pair of shoes.

I knew the feeling!

3. Find a teacher and/or group

The role of the teacher, coach, or personal trainer is regarded as critical for most practice-based learning. Whether you're wanting to learn golf or take up the piano, among your first priorities will be finding a reputable person you get along with to show you the ropes.

So, too, with meditation.

Books like this one can take you quite some way, but it's helpful to have regular access to a teacher who'll provide direction and motivation. Belonging to a group or class that meditates together regularly is also beneficial for many reasons. These include helping to normalize an activity that, initially at least, may seem somewhat foreign. When you find yourself in a group with other people you respect, it's easier to deal with your own insecurities and reservations, and focus on the practice itself.

There's also the camaraderie. Commenting on this, Meredith Fuller says, "It heightens motivation and the resulting pride in your achievement. We respond well to cues—whether that's a gold star next to your name on a noticeboard or a hug from a friend after a workout. It's far harder to let someone else down than yourself."[3]

I can't claim to have ever received a gold star or a hug from a fellow meditator after going to class—that's more for the folks in lycra—but a different and no less powerful feeling of being part of a bigger community occurs when you regularly meditate in a group.

There's also the very practical benefit of being able to talk about your own experience or concerns with fellow practitioners who are a bit further down the road than you. It's unlikely you'll encounter an obstacle others haven't. Often, it's not about the practice itself anyway, but more your feelings about the practice. It's profoundly reassuring to know you're not alone in trying to tame the mad monkey of your mind, but rather you're part of a living tradition that goes back several millennia and right now encompasses a growing number of people around the world.

Where do you find out about meditation groups? There's one website I always recommend because it seems pretty comprehensive: www.buddhanet.net. It provides lists of centers throughout the world, although these are necessarily Buddhist. For secular alternatives, a short time searching online should help.

If you live in an isolated place, far removed from the nearest teacher or center, the number of virtual alternatives is mind-boggling. You'll find many groups offering live webcasts, downloadable teachings, interactive bulletin boards, and other features. All of these help make it possible to enjoy some of the benefits of being part of a wider community.

The value of having a teacher and a group of fellow students is emphasized in Buddhism, which has done so much to keep meditation a living tradition. For these groups, what distinguishes a Buddhist from a non-Buddhist is taking refuge in the Buddha, Dharma, and Sangha. In this context "taking refuge" broadly means placing your trust in the historical Buddha as a source of wisdom, his teachings (Dharma) as instructions, and the community of fellow practitioners (Sangha) as fellow travelers on the path. It's no accident that these are much the same objects of refuge you'll find in other practice-based learning environments such as the music school, the golf club, or the gym. As one of my teachers, Zasep Tulku Rinpoche, has said, "Buddha is inspiration. Dharma is inspiration. Sangha is inspiration."

When learning to meditate, we need all the inspiration, motivation, and support we can get. Finding a teacher and/or a group is a great start, but it has to be the right teacher and group for you. We all have our own different preferences, opinions, and proclivities. Just because someone runs a meditation class doesn't make it the best choice for you. If your first efforts to find a teacher you can relate to don't succeed, try again. Take every bit as much care as you would tracking down the right accountant, builder, or GP. Your personal transformation depends on it!

4. Declare your goal

Depending on your circumstances, it may also help to declare your goal so that your nearest and dearest will hold you accountable to it. If you're living alone or with people who are unlikely to be supportive of the idea, this suggestion won't be relevant. But for many people, the knowledge that they've told their partner, colleagues, and/or housemate they're going to meditate for six weeks can, in itself, create a positive impetus to help sustain their practice.

5. Pick your battles

Starting to meditate is not a good time to also start a new diet and/or go to the gym. The idea of becoming a completely new you may, on some level, have an emotional appeal, but on any given day we draw on the same limited supply of willpower for many unrelated tasks. Developing greater willpower is the subject of the book *Willpower* by Roy F. Baumeister and John Tierney, which I wholeheartedly recommend to anyone interested in cultivating positive habits—such as meditating— or breaking negative ones. In *Willpower* they explain how every time we make a decision, such as foregoing our usual mid-morning snack, choosing a glass of water at our desk instead of coffee, and staying on the cross trainer for a full 30 minutes, our willpower is depleted, making it less likely we'll have enough in the tank to stretch to the next task requiring self-control:

This depletion isn't intuitively obvious, especially when it comes to appreciating the impact of making decisions. Virtually no one has a gut-level sense of just how tiring it is to decide. Choosing what to have for dinner, where to go on vacation, whom to hire, how much to spend—these all take willpower. Even hypothetical decisions deplete energy. After making some tough decisions, remember that your self-control is going to be weakened.[4]

In Tibetan Buddhism there's a related and amusing morality tale about a monk who arrives in an isolated village late one afternoon. In Tibet it was traditional for house-holders to provide accommodation to monks on their travels. An attractive single lady offers him a bed at her place for the night. Fearing for his vow of celibacy, the monk politely declines. When she offers him a meal, he declines that too, concerned that he might be compromised on his vow to abstain from meat. "Well, at least stay for some *chang*," she proposes, offering some of her homemade rice beer. Alcohol is also on the blacklist, but having depleted his willpower in turning down her two previous offers, he accepts—just the one drink.

Of course, you know what happens next. The first drink leads to a second, then a third, then yak stew followed by a night of unbridled passion.

So, pick your battles. Don't attempt other willpower-depleting activities when you begin meditating. And stay off the *chang*!

6. Meditate in a clean and ordered environment

Geshe Loden, my revered teacher and one of the last "old-school" lamas in the West, wrote extensive instructions on how to meditate, including several preparatory practices. The first of these is to ensure the room in which you're about to meditate is clean, "as if you were about to receive a visit from important people." Geshe-la quotes the Buddha himself as teaching the benefits of this practice, starting with the fact that your mind is "brighter, lighter, and clearer" in a clean and tidy environment. It helps prevent mental dullness and apathy: "Holding a pure motivation while cleaning causes the mind to become pure."[5]

It would be easy to dismiss this as rather quaint if well-intentioned advice of little relevance to twenty-first-century life, but recent studies dramatically show otherwise. There's a demonstrable relationship between external order and inner self-control.

In one study, two groups of participants were shown into starkly different rooms. One was neat and pristine, the other untidy and chaotic. In both rooms they were offered the same range of food and drinks from healthier options such as apples and milk to unhealthier options such as fizzy soft drinks and lollies. More people in the clean room opted for the healthy options than their counterparts in the room like the pigsty. People in the messier room also scored lower on a number of self-control metrics, including being willing to wait for more money rather than receive a smaller amount immediately—a classic test of emotional intelligence.

A separate experiment showed greater self-control and more willingness to donate to charity among users of a neat and tidy website compared to one that had exactly the same content but was messy and contained spelling errors.

What we can take out of this is that even if we don't think a chaotic bedroom or dusty surfaces have any bearing on what we're doing, external cues have a subtle but profound effect on our mind. It's easier to concentrate in a clean and ordered environment.

7. Give yourself the "nothing alternative"

As we saw in the first chapter of this book, apart from sex we find it difficult to focus on any one thing for even ten minutes. Which is why, even though you may have found a teacher, joined a group, told everyone you're giving meditation a try, and have gone to some lengths to get your room looking nice and tidy, you may still, three long minutes into your first session, decide you'd be better off checking your email inbox. You promise yourself you'll do a full ten-minute session tomorrow.

Mark Twain once wrote that the hardest part about being a writer was keeping the seat of your pants attached to the seat of the chair. Raymond Chandler concurred, devising his own "nothing alternative" rule for professional writers. In a modern reading this suggests that if writers don't feel like writing, they don't have to—but they can't do anything else, such as checking emails, surfing the net, or making a cup of coffee.

In *Willpower*, Baumeister and Tierney point out how this nothing alternative is a powerful tool against procrastination of all kinds. First, we're giving ourselves genuine choice—we don't have to meditate, we can just sit and daydream if we like. Paradoxically, the offer of this pointless activity makes us more likely to choose to focus.

The nothing alternative also embodies two techniques helpful for cultivating habits. One is that we have set a clear, unmistakable boundary where, although we don't have to meditate, we definitely won't do anything else. The other is the notion of "pre-commitment," where we're keeping temptation at bay. Yes, we may feel the tug of online status updates, but we have pre-committed to meditation or nothing for ten minutes.

One of the happiest discoveries we make as meditators is that when our focus on the object of meditation is strong, the meditation session is not only profoundly peaceful, it also flies by. As this becomes a more common experience, as is inevitable with practice, we no longer require so much will-power to meditate. We've created a habit.

8. Monitor your progress

Keeping track of your new meditation activity is another possible tool to help turn the new pursuit into a habit. Research has shown that the act of monitoring in itself helps reinforce desired behavior—if we make a note of absolutely everything we spend our money on, we're less likely to spend it on non-essential items, and to stay within our designated budget.

In the same way, simply knowing that the row of check marks in our diary—indicating the days on which we have meditated—will be broken, can exert a helpful influence to keep us on track. And if life does get in the way and we miss out, seeing all the previous check marks in our diary can help stop us giving up on ourselves as beyond hope: we did it before, we've started putting down roots, we can do it again.

9. Reward yourself

While a more mindful life is ultimately its own incalculably rich reward, in the early days you may also like to build in external rewards. A Monday-to-Friday stretch without missing a meditation session may merit a new book, a slice of chocolate cake with your coffee, half an hour walking by the sea—whatever is appropriate to your lifestyle and budget. You may decide that meditating on seven out of ten days is worthy of a reward, or twenty days in your first month as a meditator.

Having set yourself a target and a reward, don't cheat yourself once you've earned it. Take the time to reflect on your achievement and enjoy it, because it *is* an achievement. When you start out, focusing single-mindedly on your breath for ten minutes is one of the most challenging activities you'll ever have attempted. You need time and experience using the tools of mindfulness and awareness. Use whatever psychological resources you have to help you build those meditation muscles, including rewards.

10. Don't catastrophize

You started off well but then missed a day. Which became two. Then before you knew it, three. By now you haven't meditated for a stretch. Is there any point starting again?

In a word, yes. Missing a day, or even ten days, is not a catastrophe. In fact it's fairly normal. Instead you need to guard against what psychologist Albert Ellis described as one of our typical irrational beliefs, namely: "I must be absolutely competent and achieving in all important respects or else I am inadequate and worthless."

When this belief is expressed in such deliberately extreme terms, its absurdity is starkly apparent. When we start giving up on ourselves, we attract related negative thoughts, such as "I was no good at it anyway" and "I'm not cut out for meditating." Before we know it, those analytical parts of our brain are chattering away mischievously to our insula, dragging us into an unhappy negative spiral.

So don't catastrophize. You missed a few days. Whoop-de-doo. That doesn't mean you're starting again from square one, only that it's time to redouble your efforts and stay the course.

Review the benefits of meditation again, if that will help bolster your motivation. Remind yourself why you're doing this. I personally know sufferers of attention deficit disorder who learned to meditate—and have benefited enormously as a result. If they can do it, so can you. But be gentle with yourself. One step at a time.

In essence

Getting into the habit of meditating is the start of a mindfulness journey that will not only deliver the benefits outlined in the last chapter, but can take you far beyond. In time it will enable you to experience directly and first hand your ultimate nature.

But how do we sustain the benefits of our meditation practice so they flow throughout the day?

7

How to apply mindfulness in your daily life

Speed, distraction, and instant gratification are the
enemies of nearly everything that matters most in our
lives. Creating long-term value—for ourselves and for
others—requires more authentic connection, reflection,
and the courage to delay immediate gratification.
That's wisdom in action.

TONY SCHWARTZ, PRESIDENT,
THE ENERGY PROJECT[1]

Within a short time of taking up regular meditation practice, you'll start to notice changes. Science shows that the impact of meditation is immediate, even for first-time meditators, in areas from brain activity to hormone production, but because these are beneath the threshold of our awareness, we don't notice them.

What we may notice is a greater awareness of what we're thinking. Rather than being completely caught up in thoughts themselves, we may have moments of greater objectivity about what's going on in our minds and, with that, the ability to redirect or let go of our inner narrative.

We may observe ourselves becoming stressed out and frustrated by a situation, which opens up the possibility of removing ourselves from it or trying to deal with things differently. We may sometimes, for no particular reason, really enjoy looking out at a view, sipping a glass of wine, or simply being wherever we are. Little by little we create space in our minds, shift more into the direct state, and see both ourselves and the world around us with greater clarity.

In Chapter 2, I described how meditation is to a mindful life what going to the gym is to a fit life. The one supports the other. But it's by no means the whole story.

To return to the gym example, after a few weeks of working on, say, the cross trainer, the forty-something man who wants to lose weight becomes aware, perhaps for the first time in his life, of how much effort is required to burn off how many calories. Away from the gym, this fresh awareness starts to influence his behavior. Instead of ordering the sugar-loaded fizzy drink with his lunch, he may choose sparkling water. Rather than waiting for the lift to go up three floors, he'll take the stairs. Going to the gym has a ripple effect across his life, creating new habits. Increasingly he thinks of himself as a fit and healthy person, and acts accordingly.

So, too, with meditation. After getting into the habit of meditating, we become aware, perhaps for the first time in our lives, of just how agitated our minds are—but how much happier, healthier, and more efficient we are in the here and now. Away from the meditation cushion, this experience begins to influence other aspects of our behavior. Instead of being slaves to our cell phones, we find we're able to go out—or even stay in—without the constant compulsion to check for emails and updates. Rather than getting irritated by the need to wait at traffic lights or by public transport delays, we use such unexpected opportunities to tune in to the present moment. Little by little, meditation starts to affect our whole experience of reality. We become calmer and more attentive.

The changes are subtle to begin with—and for that reason we may not even be aware of them happening. But if we continue to reinforce our practice, the choices we make will inevitably lead to more far-reaching changes. We may come to enjoy the fact that even though we're more effective in our worldly pursuits, we actually require less to be happy, now we're no longer so beholden to a compulsive inner narrative. All it takes is a single cushion in a quiet room and we can reconnect to our own wellspring of profound well-being.

In the last chapter I mentioned the importance of picking your battles and not trying to make too many changes in your life at once. Once you're into the habit of a daily meditation session, there are many other tools you can use to help broaden your mindfulness practice from a single, formal session to a state of being that percolates through your whole day.

I've listed a number of suggestions below.

Spot meditation or incidental mindfulness

On even our busiest days, there are moments when we're forced to put life on hold: sitting in a meeting room waiting for colleagues to arrive; enduring minutes of piped music before a call-center operator picks up the phone. Instead of feeling frustrated about time being wasted, leaving us even fewer precious moments to do all that needs to be done, we can reframe these as opportunities for spot meditation.

As the name suggests, this is meditation we can do on the spot, in just about any situation. We don't have to get into a formal sitting meditation pose, but simply sit with a straight back, gazing at something in the mid-distance or with eyes unfocused, and breathe mindfully. The act of bringing our attention back to the breath is an effective opponent to the narrative current that usually pervades our reality. It's also a swift way to return us to the same state of calm we experience during our regular meditation practice.

Mindful breathing, even for as little as half a minute, can be a powerful way to reset our minds, let go of stress, and make us better prepared for whatever challenges we face.

There's a set of traffic lights close to where I live where I often find myself having to wait for more than two minutes. I know. I've timed the red lights, and subjectively it feels like an eternity. Since I chose to reframe the experience as an opportunity for mindfulness, fixing my gaze on the traffic light and just focusing on my breath, I no longer feel resentful or tense as I approach the lights. Quite the opposite: I look forward to simply breathing.

And is it my imagination, or are the lights more likely to be green these days, ever since I changed my attitude to them?

A few deep breaths

Even if you have only thirty seconds or less, you can shift into direct mode with a few deep breaths. Fill your lungs and, as you exhale, feel you are letting go of whatever anxieties, stress, or unhappy thoughts you may be experiencing. Just be in the moment. Breathing in and breathing out.

The effect of three deep, mindful breaths can be quite remarkable!

Cell phone mindfulness alert

If you have a mobile device with a choice of alerts, set one to go off randomly during the day, preferably with a pleasing sound or melody. That's your mindfulness alert. Whatever you're doing, try to do it more mindfully. If you're driving, just drive. If you're walking, just walk. Try to let go of the unrelated mental narrative that accompanies our actions 47 percent of the time, and focus on the actions themselves.

The colored dot technique

Most office supply shops sell small multicolored adhesive dots for file labels. The mindfulness practitioner has a different use for these stickers. Place one on your computer monitor, watch strap, fridge door, mirror, car dashboard, or any other place to remind you—just like the cell phone alert—simply to attend to the present moment.

Waking up and going to sleep

These two periods of transition can be important in setting us up for a positive day or a restful night's sleep. Yet so often we ignore the opportunity they provide.

When waking, before getting out of bed or even opening your eyes, see if you can spend a few moments simply becoming aware of your body, the sensation as you inhale and exhale.

My teacher sometimes talks about the importance of starting the day in a positive frame of mind. If you typically wake up feeling resentful about having to get out of bed, go to a job you dislike, or undertake disagreeable tasks, you're immediately setting yourself up for unhappiness. Instead, what about deliberately focusing on the positive? Ask yourself what you have to be thankful for. In what ways are you fortunate? Management gurus call this "appreciative inquiry" and it puts things on a more positive footing, whether on a personal or an organizational basis.

Similarly, when going to sleep, rather than smoldering over a hurtful exchange during the day, it would be more beneficial for a calm state of mind to reflect on your positive actions and encounters—including, of course, your formal and incidental practice of mindfulness.

I'm often asked if meditation is a good idea to do before drifting off to sleep. My questioners worry that if they do this, then when they sit on their cushions they'll nod off out of habit. In fact, a mindful state is very helpful last thing at night, especially if, like me, your mind goes all over the place as you lie there waiting to fall asleep. To go back to basics, when we're being mindful, we're paying attention to the present moment, deliberately and non-judgementally. Instead of being caught up in the narrative state—one in which our mad monkey mind scampers uncontrollably from subject to subject while we long for sleep—if we can focus on just our breath, for example, we put ourselves into a state that's much more conducive to rest.

In the Tibetan Buddhist tradition we're encouraged to go to sleep with a calm and focused mind. This isn't seen as creating an obstacle to alert and lucid practice during the day.

Relishing the pleasant

Every day most of us do sensuously enjoyable things. Ironically, we rob ourselves of the full pleasure of our sensuous enjoyments because our minds are elsewhere. Most people already possess the causes for many pleasures, but don't stop to enjoy them. We sit *in the coffee shop* drinking a $4.50 cup of coffee and, instead of tuning in to our taste buds with forensic appreciation, we take out our phone or tablet and start reading or texting, more or less ignoring our drink after the first few swallows. Where's the value for money in that?

We'll prepare *an evening meal* after a long hard day and, far from relaxing to savor the medley of textures and flavors, we turn on the TV for the latest bulletin of global tragedy and terror. Not exactly a great aid to digestion.

We'll stand *in the shower*, lathering ourselves with perhaps quite exotically scented soaps and shampoos, but we're hardly aware of the fragrances or the delightful rain of warm water on our skin—we're too busy thinking about what we're going to do next.

And so on.

You may find it useful to earmark just one of these events, or others like them, as an opportunity to practice mindfulness. From now on, when you drink coffee you're going to drink coffee. That doesn't mean you can't also read the paper. It does mean that each time you raise the cup to your mouth, take a sip, savor the flavor, and then swallow, you'll focus exclusively on just that.

Even the subtlest changes can make a big difference to our experience of reality. When we enjoy a meal, that enjoyment has a much greater impact than if we'd merely consumed the food while doing something else. We haven't changed what we've done, only the way we've done it.

If our purpose in life is to be happy, before looking for new causes of happiness, it makes sense first to identify the happiness-creating experiences we already have in our lives, and to leverage them using mindfulness.

Making neutral experiences more interesting

As well as turning up the volume on enjoyable activities, mindfulness can also be used to make the myriad of daily neutral experiences more interesting. These include shaving; brushing our teeth; doing our hair and make-up; getting dressed; walking to and from the car, station, or office; driving the car; going to the toilet; washing our hands; and so on. Mostly, we do these things on autopilot, all the while thinking about something else.

Here's an idea: designate at least one of these a mindfulness activity. Turn it into an opportunity to punctuate your narrative day with a short time in the direct state.

By now you have a good idea what's needed. The challenge is to experience what's happening in real time without judgement, resisting your usual impulse to get caught up in mental commentary about either what's happening or something completely different.

You're not expecting some kind of epiphany as you floss your teeth. Nor should you hope to emerge from the lavatory in a state of Zen-like calm. But without taking time out of your schedule you're creating the subjective experience of having more time. The more we live in the direct state, the more interest and depth we discover, even in the mundane.

Transforming chores

Most of us would have little difficulty listing the chores we'd happily relinquish for the rest of our lives: washing dishes and ironing clothes, mowing the lawn and weeding the garden, vacuuming the house, cleaning cars, and any number of other tedious domestic duties. Unless we can afford household staff, we're pretty much stuck with these. So, in the interests of our own personal happiness, we just have to make the best of them.

Mindfulness helps us do just this. In Chapter 4 I described research from Duke University's Center for Mindfulness Research and the University of Oregon's Music Department, which showed that music seemed more enjoyable to people who meditated. The practice of mindfulness had the effect of renewing even the most jaded responses to pieces of music that had been heard too many times already. This willingness to experience what happens to us from a fresh perspective is perhaps what Marcel Proust had in mind when he wrote: "The real voyage of discovery exists not in seeing new landscapes but in having new eyes."

The new eyes offered by mindfulness could be described as a willingness to give very close attention to the matter in hand, whatever it is—to notice and try to appreciate every fold of the shirt being ironed, every panel of the car being washed. Instead of doing a chore grudgingly, we adopt the curiosity of a botanist about to venture into a jungle where they strongly suspect hitherto unknown flora await discovery. What do we notice? What can we find? What is it like to simply be in this moment, here and now?

This response is the very opposite of avoidance—putting off the chore for as long as we can, then when it can be put off no more, doing it as quickly as possible, quite possibly with the radio on full blast or some other distraction to "take our mind off things"—a curious expression, given that most of us find it well-nigh impossible to keep our mind on anything.

Paradoxically, we may find the object of our tedium is actually a lot less boring than we've long assumed. We may become so engrossed and grounded in the experience that we not only forget how much we dislike it, we find ourselves absorbed in an activity that gives fresh texture to our day. If you're a cerebral type of person, and/or your job involves a lot of conceptual thinking, you may actually find mindful work in the home or garden useful, emerging from it re-created, with a calmer, clearer mind.

········· **In essence** ·········

It can sometimes feel that life passes us by in an unlived blur. "I don't know where this week/month/year has gone," runs the cliché. We'll see the first Christmas decorations appear in the shops and subjectively feel as though the last festive season is barely behind us. Running fast and hard, responding to the many imperatives that drive us, in truth we spend much of our lives in a state of frenetic mindlessness. John Lennon once famously wrote that "Life is what happens to you while you're busy making other plans."

Regular meditation practice is the foundation for a calmer, more insightful, and contented experience of reality. The suggestions in this chapter are other ways to make daily life more mindful. With practices like these we can reclaim our lives moment by moment, finding space even in the midst of hurry, creating awareness where there was little before, achieving greater control of our own mind space.

Being better.

8

Our mindfulness journey

Your present circumstances don't determine where you can go; they merely determine where you start.

DR. NIDO QUBEIN, BUSINESSMAN, AUTHOR, AND SPEAKER[1]

O ur mindfulness journey is like a river. If you've ever been in the mountains, you may have encountered trickles of water so small you can cup them in your hands. The only impact these silver ribbons have on the surrounding countryside is, perhaps, a narrow band of fine moss following their course. Sometimes the trickles disappear altogether and go underground. They may re-emerge a distance away or make an appearance in cascading waterfalls. The early part of their journey is one of fits and starts.

The streams build, joining together with other streams to form a river. The current becomes steady and smooth and on its banks grow trees and lush vegetation. Farmers and villagers may depend on that river, and its course is clearly visible from a distance. If you stand on a hill, you can see the river's impact on the landscape, how a margin of verdant life follows its passage as it unwinds across the landscape.

Joining with other tributaries, the river grows even wider and deeper. The further it goes, the more it matures, evolving until it's no longer simply an element of the scenery. It's the defining feature. It affects everything in the surrounding areas; it's a source of life, of movement, of abiding pleasure. It's the reason towns and cities are located where they are. Many of the world's great capital cities are situated on river mouths, the point where the water that started on the mountain top ultimately merges with the ocean.

Our mindfulness practice may feel modest and ineffectual when we begin. Progress may be erratic. We may give up on meditation altogether for periods. But it's my experience that once people have understood the benefits of a more mindful life and tasted them, however briefly, they'll come back.

When we supplement our meditation with other mindfulness practices we're adding tributaries, strengthening what we do. We become more acquainted with mindfulness in daily life. We still get caught up in our mindless narrative, of course, but once we've established a steady flow, we have no wish to move too far away from it for too long. We certainly don't want it to end.

Over time, mindfulness begins to affect everything in our lives: our choices about how we spend our time, who we spend it with, and what we find useful or entertaining. It shapes our whole understanding of who we are and what makes our lives happy and meaningful.

Navigating the journey

So much for the metaphor. What about the practical reality of navigating from the mountain top to the river mouth? The following table is one way of outlining broadly what to expect. Like other skill-based learning activities, the speed with which we move from stages 1 to 4 is dependent on individual effort and circumstances. But being aware of the journey helps us better prepare for it.

Stage 1	Stage 2	Stage 3	Stage 4
No skills	Some skills	More skills	Many skills
High motivation	Low motivation	Some motivation	High motivation

Stage 1

We usually begin our meditation journey with a sense of strong enthusiasm. Perhaps we've been inspired by a speaker or a book. We're convinced by the benefits of a more mindful life and we want them now! So perhaps we enroll in a class, set our alarm clock ten minutes earlier, and sprinkle colorful dots in places we can't possibly miss them.

Stage 2

At this stage we discover how agitated our minds are and how difficult the simple process of meditation actually is. We may be frustrated at our own inability to focus on just one thing. Other skills we've learned during our lives, such as driving a car, speaking a foreign language, or using new software, seem like a walk in the park compared to meditating. Many people are surprised to discover that the gentle practice of meditation is their toughest challenge ever.

This is the point at which many people put meditation in the too-hard basket. And it's for precisely this reason that I wrote the chapter on getting into a meditation habit (see Chapter 6). The motivation to get us through this stage while we work on improving our concentration is what we need more than anything.

For most of us, the best way to get motivated is through a teacher, fellow classmates, regular contact with people who inspire us, and exposure to books or videos that support our practice. YouTube and other online video services have a wealth of material for those who live too far away from centers to make frequent visits but still have good internet access. My advice is to find a source that works for you and tap into it as much as you need to sustain your practice.

Stage 3

We have made noticeable progress in our meditative concentration—perhaps now we can go for a full session without losing count of our breaths, and/or have increased our count from cycles of four breaths to cycles of ten. We have experienced some of the benefits of mindfulness personally. We don't just know the theory—we enjoy some of the benefits.

But it's still hard work. We may procrastinate and find excuses not to meditate. We'll allow major life events to torpedo our practice—often, ironically, at the very time it would help us most. For a while our river may be dammed, diverted, or disappear underground.

Again, it's motivation that will get us back to the cushion and through this stage. We may have many more skills than before, and our practice may be steadier, but meditation is still not the calm, flowing center of our lives. We may need help getting back on course, but when we do, our practice resumes. We discover that our previous effort wasn't wasted. We resume our course with a fresh appreciation for the peace it brings.

···················· *Stage 4* ····················

Somewhere along the line, we find that we no longer require regular pep talks and encouragement. We've not only heard it all before, we've integrated it into our lives, and the additional exploration and reading we've done for ourselves makes us more self-sufficient in our practice.

The idea of not meditating is now deeply unappealing. Not only do we actually enjoy our sessions, we're all too aware of how unpleasant we feel when we don't meditate ("Is this how we used to feel all the time?" we ask ourselves incredulously). Sure, we can go a day or two without a formal session if we find ourselves traveling. We can confine our practice to a few snatched sessions on an airplane seat. But meditation is both a priority and a pleasure. We'd frankly much rather sit in a quiet room alone than take part in banal socializing or watch some hackneyed TV re-run. Competent and motivated, we're ready to explore the furthermost frontiers of our mind.

The tributaries of mindfulness

As established at the beginning of this book, a strong meditation practice is the foundation of a more mindful life. Meditation supports our enhanced awareness of the here and now, greater mindfulness in our interactions with others, and a more profound appreciation of everyday life. But while meditation is like the river in our analogy, there are additional tributaries—other mindfulness practices that contribute to the development of the river from a faltering stream in the early stages to a steadier and more important part of our lives until, eventually, we experience reality, 24/7, in a mindful state.

The practices outlined in the previous chapter are the tributaries of the river. When we bring additional moments of mindfulness to the central flow of our regular meditation— mindfully drinking a cup of coffee, waiting at the traffic lights, washing the car, enjoying a shower—we strengthen our capacity to dwell in direct mode. Little by little we begin to abandon the self-focused narrative that so rarely serves us well and embrace instead the habit of abiding in the here and now—the only place happiness can be found.

Managing expectations

Meditation and mindfulness are a lifetime's practice. In a world where the search for gratification is ever more impatient, where we get irritated if our computer screen doesn't refresh in a couple of seconds, our attitude towards both meditation and mindfulness needs to be very different. In particular, we have to retain a focus on the "nonjudgmental" part of the mindfulness definition.

In meditation, thoughts arise quite naturally out of mind in just the same way that waves emerge from the ocean. That's the way of things. There'll be days, weeks, even months when we experience higher levels of agitation and may feel we're "not making progress." In mindfulness, we may agree with ourselves that, henceforth, every time we drink a barista-made coffee we'll fully engage our powers of taste and smell . . . then two days later we realize we've paid hardly any attention to a near-empty cup of cappuccino.

This is time not to berate ourselves but to practice self-compassion. If ever there was a practice that was more about the journey than the destination, meditation is it. Sure, our goal is to pay attention to the present moment, but if we find we've slipped into narrative mode, we simply and patiently return our focus to the object of meditation. When we consider how many hours of every day we allow our mind unfettered roaming from one thought to the next, it would be unrealistic to expect to tame our mad monkey mind with only a short-term intervention. This is a theme to which the Dalai Lama often returns.

But we can take two things to heart. First, as the wealth of research evidence presented in Chapter 4 clearly shows, even if you don't subjectively feel that you're achieving much by meditating, the clinical reality is that you are. You're benefiting in more ways than can be imagined. There's no more powerful, positive, and holistic way to enhance your well-being.

Second, if you stick with it, over time your concentration will improve. It may happen so gradually that it escapes your attention. Do you notice how much your hair has grown overnight when you face yourself in the mirror? Of course not! But go without a haircut for six weeks, especially if you started with it short, and the change is unmistakable.

The Dalai Lama gives good advice on managing expectations:

Inner development comes step by step. You may think, "Today my calmness, my mental peace, is very small," but still, if you compare, if you look five, ten, or fifteen years back and think, "What was my way of thinking then? How much inner peace did I have then and what is it today?" Comparing it with what it was then, you can realize that there is some progress, there is some value. This is how you should compare—not with today's feeling and yesterday's feeling or last week or last month, even not last month, even not last year, but five years ago. Then you can realize what improvement has occurred internally. Progress comes by maintaining constant effort in daily practice.[2]

Meditation teacher B. Alan Wallace offers a useful metaphor when suggesting we manage our mindfulness practice like a family farm. We may plant an orchard knowing it won't bear fruit for years, but we can be sustained by seasonal crops. Our concentration may take a long time to mature, but in the meantime the daily harvest of our practice arises from an improved feeling of peacefulness, greater capacity to find happiness in the here and now, and enhanced relationships with others. In time, we'll enjoy both an abundance of fruit and the seasonal crops we become practiced at harvesting. Our journey is not only ripe with promise, but also offers us benefits from the moment we take our first step.

The nine levels of meditative concentration

Expectations duly managed, there's a yardstick we can use to identify our progress. It's called the nine levels of meditative concentration and has been with us since at least the time of the Buddha.

What I find reassuring about these levels is that the first two stages are described as those of a meditator who spends more time distracted than on the object of meditation. Agitation is the norm. There's hope for us all yet!

Level 1: Placing the mind

At this stage you spend more time during each session being distracted than focusing on the object of meditation. While you can place your mind on the object of meditation for short periods, you also become aware, perhaps for the first time, of the full extent of your mental agitation. There's only one way from here and it's up!

Level 2: Placement with continuity

While most of your meditation session is still distracted, you can sometimes hold the object of concentration for two minutes or more before being interrupted by gross agitation or dullness.

Level 3: Patch-like placement

The balance of your meditation sessions has changed so that the majority of your time is now spent engaged with your chosen object of meditation. Also, when you lose the object through distraction or dullness, you find it easier to resume concentration than you used to, as your mindfulness is improving.

Level 4: Close placement

Your meditative concentration continues to improve to the point that, while you still experience periods of agitation and/or dullness, you can now hold the object of meditation over longer periods of time—between five and ten minutes.

Level 5: Controlling

You can now meditate for an entire session without your concentration being disrupted by gross agitation or dullness, but you still experience subtle agitation and/or dullness. Subtle dullness is the particular challenge.

Level 6: Pacifying

At this stage you can not only meditate for an entire session without your concentration being disturbed, you also experience only a small degree of subtle agitation and/or dullness. Subtle agitation is the particular challenge of this level.

Level 7: Complete pacification

Your concentration has improved to the point that if any subtle agitation and dullness arise you can quickly overcome them through your greatly increased power of concentration.

Level 8: Single-pointed concentration

You can now hold the object of meditation completely throughout the session, with only slight effort required at the beginning.

Level 9: Placement with equanimity

In this final stage you can concentrate on an object of meditation for any length of time without effort.

Just in case any residual suspicions that meditation requires an innate talent are still lurking in the more skeptical recesses of your mind, the findings of psychologist K. Anders Ericsson and two Florida State University colleagues from studies conducted at Berlin's Academy of Music are worthy of reflection. Together with the academy's professors, Ericsson's team looked at violinists and pianists, whom they graded into different categories. In the highest category were the world-class soloists—those who might perform on stage backed by a full symphony orchestra or in solo recital. Next were those who were good enough to play in such orchestras. In the lowest level were musicians who were unlikely to play professionally but might become teachers.[3]

Music is one of many activities in which some people appear to be naturally gifted. Most of us can think of kids with whom we were at school who seemed to be able to pick up just about any instrument and make a great sound from it. They were effortless performers, be it on the piano, guitar, or mouth organ. The idea that everyone would have been equally able as them to have a crack at a Shostakovich Piano Concerto by the time they left school would have seemed plain crazy.

But here's the extraordinary thing. Ericsson and his colleagues found that although all the academy's violinists had started out playing for around two or three hours a day when they were very young, by about the age of eight, the students who would end up in the top category started practicing much more than anyone else. And they kept on increasing the hours they practiced. So much so that by the age of twenty, no one in the most elite group had totalled fewer than 10,000 hours. The next group down had all put in at least 8,000 hours. The future music teachers had practiced for at least 4,000 hours.[4]

This same 10,000-hour trend held true for both violinists and pianists. Writing in *This Is Your Brain on Music: The Science of a Human Obsession*, neurologist Daniel J. Levitin notes, "In study after study, of composers, basketball players, fiction writers, ice skaters, concert pianists, chess players, master criminals, and what have you, this number comes up again and again . . . No one has yet found a case in which true world-class expertise was accomplished in less time."[5]

Exploring the 10,000-hour rule in his book *Outliers*, Malcolm Gladwell makes the point that no musical "naturals" floated to the top category, able to cruise in having done fewer hours because of an innate talent. Conversely, no one who put in the hours failed to make it to the relevant category because they weren't gifted enough.[6]

Meditation conforms to precisely the same principles. It isn't about an innate talent or natural gift, it's about applying the seat of your pants to the meditation cushion. No one has some kind of head start on you, nor are you handicapped by an especially agitated mind. If there is such a thing as a "talent" for mindfulness—or music, basketball, or ice-skating—it would seem to be nothing more than an enthusiasm for the practice. And the more you practice, the more talented you become!

Mindfulness and ethics

At a seminar I presented to a business group some time ago, I was asked an especially insightful question: "Does the practice of meditation encourage people to behave more ethically?"

As it happens, there's an interesting analogy to illustrate this very point. It runs along the lines that for someone who doesn't practice meditation, unethical behavior is like a hair falling on the open palm of the hand. For someone who practices meditation, the same behavior is like a hair falling on the eyeball—that is, it's intolerable.

In repeating this analogy I'm not for one moment suggesting that the vast majority of people whom we may admire for their scrupulous integrity are somehow ethically deficient because they don't formally meditate. The importance of this metaphor is that the regular practice of meditation sensitizes us to our own thoughts, speech, and actions, and the ways these impact on others. In becoming more self-aware and attuned to our own wishes for happiness and to avoid pain, it also quite naturally becomes more obvious that others are motivated by just these same factors. Whereas before, with a mind clouded by agitation, we may have been able to overlook, discount, or justify behavior that advanced our own interests at the expense of others, when we experience greater clarity, it becomes increasingly difficult to ignore, avoid, or evade the ways our own actions may harm others. It also becomes less acceptable to us.

One striking illustration is the impact of meditation on the re-offense rates of prisoners. Around the world, a number of programs teach meditation of different kinds in prison systems, including the Liberation Prison Project founded by Australian Buddhist nun Robina Courtin. These have demonstrated spectacular but unsurprising reductions in re-offense rates, drug and alcohol dependence, and other negative behaviors among inmates. Even in environments such as prisons, which are magnets for negativity, psychopathology, and suffering in all forms, when people are willing to undertake the simple steps that enable greater self-awareness, one consequence is the nurturing of more ethical behavior.

On an everyday and no less important basis, when we develop greater mindfulness, activities that may have passed us by before become less tolerable to us: sitting around the table bad-mouthing friends or colleagues, or even listening to others venting their spleen; sliding into duplicitous relationships that compromise the partnerships, business or personal, that we already enjoy; turning a blind eye to dodgy dealings and corruption; doing nothing to alleviate the suffering of others when even a very modest contribution of time or money could make a huge difference. These and countless other examples of unethical behavior become less acceptable to us because we find that they disturb our peace of mind.

It would be a tough ask to sit down to a meditation session hoping to enjoy a state of meditative calm and equanimity if you knew your significant other was about to discover you'd been cheating on them. Transcendental bliss is unlikely to occur if you're aware that a business associate, the tax office, or another professional might find out you're engaged in an elaborate cover-up or fraud. It just isn't worth it. Increasingly, *nothing* is worth risking your peace of mind, because without peace of mind, we have nothing.

Which brings us to the counterpoint of the hair in the eyeball metaphor: just as mindfulness practice encourages the cultivation of ethical behavior, ethical behavior is an important foundation in the cultivation of mindfulness. The two are mutually supportive.

McMindfulness and the lotus

As mindfulness programs have become more popularized, almost inevitably some purists have objected to the way mind-training techniques have been stripped from their original Buddhist context, dumbed down, and packaged for the masses. A term has even been invented for the end result: McMindfulness. Exhibit A, on the part of those who prosecute this argument, is the fact that mindfulness is traditionally taught in the context of a lifestyle founded on morality and wholesome intentions. Helping someone cultivate mindfulness in order to become, for example, a more effective trained killer or a white-collar criminal isn't exactly in keeping with the spirit of things.

For reasons explained in Chapter 1, I have some reservations about the proliferation of mindfulness programs, but these center mainly on the concern that many of them don't take participants far enough down the road to experience the full benefits of the practice. I'm less concerned about people not being able to differentiate "right mindfulness" from "wrong mindfulness," because self-awareness, empathy, compassion, and a sense of community arise quite naturally as we become increasingly in touch with our own true nature. This isn't necessarily a "bolt from the sky" experience so much as a gradual awakening that sees us turning away from behaviors that are inconsistent with our inner experience and threaten our equanimity.

Our mindfulness journey is therefore one that has repercussions way beyond getting better at paying attention to the present moment deliberately and non-judgementally. It's one that leads inevitably to inner change. I've already shared several metaphors in this chapter, describing different elements of the mindfulness journey, but I'd like to share one used in Buddhism to describe the process.

The lotus is a well-known Buddhist symbol, used liberally in paintings and sculptures, but less well known is its meaning. Lotus plants typically grow in muddy water. From these inauspicious circumstances, firmly rooted in darkness and decay, the plants nevertheless grow to the surface, where they blossom into flowers of the most extraordinary and unlikely beauty.

As with most Buddhist symbols, this one may be interpreted on many different levels. But perhaps the most self-evident is that even though we may be rooted in circumstances involving hardship, negativity, or moral detritus, transcendence is still possible. It is possible for the very fact of this hardship, negativity, and moral detritus—having experienced the suffering of it, we wish to turn away from it. Like the lotus, we have the potential to rise above it, and to realize our true nature in a blossoming of peerless and exquisite radiance. This is the ultimate destination of our mindfulness journey: the realization not only of the boundless, tranquil, and benevolent nature of our own mind, but also of our purest motives and integrity. The potentiality we already possess finds its final and most authentic expression in this pristine and glorious flowering.

9

How mindfulness makes us happier

....

Happiness does not depend on outward things,
but on the way we see them.

LEO TOLSTOY

....

So far in this book we've explored a wide array of benefits arising from both meditation and mindfulness, including the way our "set point" for happiness, as measured by the activity in our left prefrontal cortex, can be shifted (see Chapter 4). Studies of the kind carried out by Drs. Richard Davidson and Jon Kabat-Zinn are immensely valuable in delivering empirical evidence that meditation helps people become calmer, healthier, and happier. But you may be wondering just *how* meditation achieves this. What is the connection between a more lucid state of mind and feelings of well-being? Why does mindfulness matter when the culture we live in so emphatically focuses on external circumstances as the true cause of happiness?

What we *think* makes us happy

If you were to stop a hundred people in the street and ask them what it takes to be happy, chances are you'd hear all the conventional answers—financial security, personal achievement, success, and a happy marriage would figure among many people's ingredients for fulfilment and well-being. Religion or beliefs may get a few mentions, and it's highly unlikely that mindfulness would feature at all.

But to what extent are any of these traditional notions of happiness reliable? Exploring them briefly helps place mindfulness in a useful context.

Money

The pursuit of money is an omnipresent motivator of human behavior. How much of what we do, plan, and think about is aimed at securing our material circumstances? As long ago as 1759, Adam Smith, the father of modern economics, explained how the idea that wealth creates happiness is an illusory belief— but one needed to keep the wheels of an economy turning:

The pleasures of wealth and greatness . . . strike the imagin-
ation as something grand and beautiful and noble, of
which the attainment is well worth all the toil and anxiety
which we are so apt to bestow upon it . . . It is this deception
which rouses and keeps in continual motion the industry of
mankind.[1]

Since then, economists and psychologists have studied the relationship between wealth and happiness. Their collective conclusion is that although wealth certainly buys happiness when it lifts people out of poverty, it does little to improve our sense of well-being thereafter. If you don't know where your next meal is coming from, haven't a place to call home, or are ill without access to medical help, then yes, money will make a very big difference to the way you feel. Generally, the person earning $70,000 a year is a lot happier than the one on $10,000.

But research consensus suggests that if you earn $1 million a year, you're not necessarily much happier than the person on $70,000. You may fly first class, drive a prestige car, and live in a salubrious suburb, but none of these things will necessarily make you happier than your more budget-conscious peers, quite simply because you get so used to earning, and spending, at that level that it has a much more limited impact on your sense of well-being.

Most of us have experienced this effect in our own way. Perhaps you can remember the thrill of acquiring your first smartphone, tablet, or other electronic wizardry. For days, possibly weeks, you marvelled at its magical capabilities. But at some point, without you even realizing, it ceased to seem so special. And after the sleeker, shinier new model was released, capable of doing twice as much in half the time, your own device started to feel decidedly passé. The device itself hadn't changed, but your attitude towards it had.

Economists use the phrase "declining marginal utility" to describe how more and more of any one thing delivers less and less. Psychologists label it "adaptation" or "habituation"—after a while, what was once extraordinary becomes so much the norm that we barely notice it.

Thinking back to the moments in our lives when we've felt most intensely alive, fulfilled, and happy, for most of us there's little correlation between these moments and peaks in our net wealth. Many people recall periods in early adulthood, perhaps living independently for the first time, as among the most vibrant of their lives. Usually these are also times of shabby accommodation, tight budgets, and cheap beer.

The behavior of some of the world's wealthiest people is also instructive. Warren Buffett and Carlos Slim Helú, two of the world's richest men, both choose to live in the same, very ordinary houses they bought decades earlier. Ingvar Kamprad, founder of Ikea, prefers economy seats and Ikea cafeterias to flying first class and upscale restaurants. What's the reason for these personal choices? Are they just curious quirks or do these ultra-affluent individuals recognize the truth of habituation?

Demand for antidepressants also presents us with a paradox. I'm told by a senior medical practitioner that prescriptions of these in my hometown of Perth, Australia, are highest in the western suburbs—the most affluent suburbs. If material comfort were a reliable cause of happiness, there would certainly be no need for antidepressants in ritzy neighborhoods!

In short, the relationship between money and happiness is much more tenuous than we generally suppose. Many of the assumptions we make about wealth simply don't bear up to scrutiny.

Achievement and status

For many of us there seems to be something almost innate about our wish to improve our standing in life, whether by way of a promotion at work, material advancement, or increased influence, a qualification, setting up a business, or perhaps some artistic or scientific achievement. But how effectively do status and its trappings enhance our sense of well-being?

Not very, according to Tim Kasser, professor of psychology at Knox College in Illinois and author of *The High Price of Materialism*, who has studied exactly this phenomenon. His research shows that people who place a high value on perceived achievement, image, and wealth tend to suffer more from depression, anxiety, and low self-worth. Professor Kasser identified two different types of goals—"extrinsic goals" focusing on materialistic values, and "intrinsic goals" focusing on personal growth, community feeling, and so on. His work shows that, far from enhancing any sense of happiness, a preoccupation with materialistic goals such as status actually perpetuates feelings of insecurity, weakening the ties that bind us to others and making us feel less free.

In some ways this extrinsic–intrinsic dichotomy looks back to Aristotle's view that hedonic activity—when we seek pleasure by taking from the world—delivers only short-term happiness. On the other hand, eudemonic activity—when we seek happiness by giving to the world—delivers a far more enduring and profound sense of well-being. True happiness, according to Aristotle, was "an activity of the soul in accordance with virtue."[2]

Research reported in *Forbes* magazine shows that in the working world, perceived success and status have nothing to do with job satisfaction. Factors such as being in control of what we do, work relationships, and company culture are far more important. Looking through the lens of achievement and prestige, you may expect a lawyer to be happier than, or at least level-pegging with, a real estate agent. But in a CareerBliss survey of more than 65,000 people in the United States, real estate agents reported the highest levels of job satisfaction with an index score of 4.26 out of 5, while associate attorneys were rock bottom on 2.89. It seems there's nothing about being a rocket scientist, brain surgeon, presidential adviser, or any other high-status job that makes it inherently more fulfilling.[3]

If status itself doesn't do it, what of the trappings of status? Can they help compensate for the fact that it can be tough at the top?

I'll never forget my incredulity, being inducted as a graduate trainee at a bank headquarters, when it was explained to me that the size of office potted plants was determined by job title. An image instantly came to mind of a white-coated plant auditor doing the rounds every week, tape measure and shears in one hand and organizational chart in the other, ensuring that no one's foliage outgrew their position on the corporate hierarchy. The reality was no doubt more prosaic, but it was the first time I became aware than even a potted plant could be coopted as a marker of corporate importance!

Status symbols usually involve items a lot more luxurious than leafy aspidistras. Whether it's cars, clothes, or kitchen appliances, there's no end to the trinkets and baubles with which people signal to others that they're moving up in the world, and which fall into the category of what Cornell University economist Robert Frank labels "conspicuous consumption." "Inconspicuous consumption," by contrast, is those things we value for themselves, such as time spent with family and friends.

In his book *Luxury Fever*, Frank outlines the mistake we make when we value conspicuous over inconspicuous consumption in our search for happiness. In the USA he suggests that instead of large houses in the suburbs with long commutes to work, we'd be a lot happier with smaller houses and shorter commutes, enabling us more time to spend with family and friends, or doing whatever else we find personally fulfilling. Similarly, accepting lower pay but taking longer holidays would probably also support our happiness more effectively than higher pay but very little downtime.[4]

Frank argues that conspicuous consumption separates us from other people. Many of us have first-hand experience of feeling dislocated from people who self-consciously occupy a very different status from ours. They may not live in a different world, but because of their trappings and, importantly, the way they relate to them, it can certainly feel that way. This is true of people who are fixated on status, whether they're much further up or down any particular totem pole, be it politics, celebrity, or car choice.

By contrast, inconspicuous consumption is what draws us together. It's about time spent together, playing sports, performing music, going for a morning swim. Here the emphasis is on the things we have in common, and which, once the assumed personas of status are dropped, are so much more important than those things that separate us.

Love and so on

Even before "love and marriage" was found to scan neatly with "horse and carriage," relationships have been regarded as the foundation of a happy life. Whole genres of music, books, TV shows, and magazines are devoted to tales of romantic and sexual intimacy. More specifically, the growth of weddings from religious ceremonies to big business over the past decades attests to the dreams and dollars invested when couples commit to living happily ever after.

There's no shortage of research showing that committed relationships correlate positively not only with happiness but also with good health. But as psychology professor Sonja Lyubomirsky of the University of California, Riverside, points out, the marriage and happiness correlation is a two-way street, because it's also the case that happier people are more likely to attract and retain a partner.

The idea of being in a relationship and/or married is one that appeals to most of us, and research suggests we *do* get a substantial boost from being married . . . but that this loving feeling tends to last an average of around two years. Thereafter, we don't automatically experience any more happiness than our single peers from one moment to the next.

Writing for *Psychology Today*, Professor Lyubomirsky cites a study that tracked a number of married women hour by hour, revealing that marriage confers both costs as well as benefits—and that these seemed to offset each other. Yes, married women may have less time on their own, but they also spend more time doing housework, preparing food, and tending to children, and less time with friends, reading books, or watching TV.[5]

Professor Lyubomirsky concludes that while there's no doubt that strong, warm interpersonal relationships make us happy, these relationships need not be sexual or marital. Close friendships or family relationships also offer happiness.

Let's talk about sex. Mr. Wilkins, the biology teacher at the all-boys school I attended, was famous for delivering the same human reproduction lecture each year to his sixteen-year-old pupils: if you put a marble in a large jar every time you had sex in your first year of marriage, Mr. Wilkins would explain in his chipper British accent, and then removed a marble from that same jar every time you had sex from the second year onwards, you'd never exhaust the marbles.

There were, to be fair, certain assumptions baked into this model—the absence of both pre-marital sex and Viagra among them—but of course none of us believed Mr. Wilkins and his jar theory. We would mimic his words and caricature his delivery without mercy. As a middle-aged man in a beige safari suit and lime knee-high socks, what did he know about sex? As far as we hormonally charged teenagers were concerned, it didn't seem remotely possible to exhaust the fantasy of a permanently sexually available partner.

Decades later, as middle-aged men ourselves, albeit sans the safari suit, we know he was simply referring to the Coolidge effect—the tendency for many species to tire of the same sexual partner but to show renewed interest when new, receptive sexual partners become available. The term is derived from an anecdote about an occasion on which US president Calvin Coolidge visited a farm. When his wife, who accompanied him, came to the chicken yard, she noticed that a rooster was mating very frequently. She asked the attendant how often that happened and was told, "Dozens of times each day." Mrs. Coolidge said, "Tell that to the president when he comes by." Upon being told, Coolidge asked, "Same hen every time?"

The reply was, "Oh, no, Mr. President, a different hen every time." President Coolidge said, "Tell that to Mrs. Coolidge."[5]

The Coolidge effect neatly encapsulates the conflict of biological drives and monogamous relationships. It describes how even an instinct as powerful as sex can become the subject of habituation—and why, after fifty years of marriage, people may still have at least some of their marbles!

What about children as a source of happiness? Most of us with children would unhesitatingly name our kids as the most important thing in our lives. We'd put them before us and do just about anything to help them. Aren't they life's richest blessing?

Professor Daniel Gilbert stirred up something of a hornet's nest in his insightful book *Stumbling on Happiness* by suggesting otherwise. In particular, he revealed four separate research programs showing that couples who started married life happily together become dramatically less happy after their first child appeared. Decreased satisfaction continued as children grew to become teenagers, but happiness levels soared once the children left home. This trend was stronger for women than men, and studies show that mothers generally feel happier when eating, exercising, shopping, napping, or watching television than when taking care of their children. In fact, child care seems only marginally more pleasant for them than doing the housework.[7]

Why we believe that money, success, and relationships make us happy

When both our own subjective experience and the growing weight of research call into question the reliability of money, material achievements, and familial relationships to deliver happiness, why do we persist in holding these beliefs?

Professor Gilbert offers an intriguing explanation about belief transmission. If a belief has a particular quality that facilitates its own transmission, it will be held by an increasing number of minds, even when that belief is untrue: "False beliefs that happen to promote stable societies tend to propagate because people who hold these beliefs tend to live in stable societies, which provide the means by which false beliefs propagate."[8]

For societies to thrive, we need citizens who are economically productive, those with the highest skills to be retained, people to get married and procreate, thereby providing the next generation, and men not to upset the social apple cart by behaving like Mrs. Coolidge's rooster. No surprise, then, that notions of money, status, and marriage providing the basis of a happy life are so deeply entrenched.

Or so explicit. We're bombarded daily with appeals to change the external landscape of our lives. Every advertisement we absorb holds out the promise of greater happiness if we drive a particular car, use a specific brand of tampon, or wear an exclusive design of jewelry. The desirability of upgrading our material circumstances, and keeping Adam Smith's motion of industry rolling forward, is implicit all around us in TV dramas and reality shows, media reports and Facebook updates—the assumed conviction being that we all aspire to similar external goals.

Large tranches of the self-help industry must also take responsibility not only for encouraging beliefs that wealth, abundance, and romantic love are reliable sources of happiness, but also for propagating subsidiary beliefs—for example, that we all deserve such things in abundance, that the only things stopping us from having them are self-limiting notions and that the universe will give us whatever we ask. From Napoleon Hill's classic *Think and Grow Rich* to Rhonda Byrne's more recent law of attraction–based *The Secret*, ideas that the floodgates of abundance will open with the daily recitation of the right affirmation continue to be as popular as they are problematic.

Books like these may certainly help with the very real problems of self-doubt, woolly thinking, and poor motivation, but in encouraging people to believe that happiness is to be found in growing rich, self-help gurus may be propelling their followers only more effectively in the wrong direction.

If happiness is the objective, and wealth is merely a means to that objective, why not explain how to reach the objective directly?

Where conventional beliefs about happiness go awry is in assuming a direct, causal relationship between something outside us—a beautiful home, car, or spouse—and a feeling of happiness.

In reality, no direct relationship exists. Buddhists have a word for the mistaken view that outer and inner are directly connected—"superstition." It's as superstitious, for example, to believe that thinking and growing rich will make you happy as it is to believe that a breaking mirror foreshadows seven years of bad luck.

One of Buddha's central teachings was that no person, object, or situation has inherent qualities that deliver happiness. Rather, it's our minds that perceive happiness-giving qualities. And as we all know, minds are prone to change.

Buddhist teachers are fond of setting their students a particular challenge: go and find the person or object that's a reliable cause of happiness and bring him, her, or it back so that we can all share the love. By "reliable cause" we mean something or someone who unfailingly produces happiness in the same way as, for example, heat applied to water will always eventually produce steam, no matter where it happens, when it happens, or how many times it might have happened already.

Our recognition that no such happiness-providing person or thing exists helps deepen our understanding of where both happiness and unhappiness really come from . . . and it's not "out there."

Stoic philosophers, one of the strongest influences on western philosophy, arrived around the third century BC at a recognition similar to Buddha. In *Meditations*, Roman emperor Marcus Aurelius observed: "If you are distressed by anything external, the pain is not due to the thing itself, but to your estimate of it; and this you have the power to revoke at any moment."[9]

The cognitive behavior model

Much more recently in the West, cognitive behavior therapy has described the relationship between external reality and our feelings in the ways outlined in the table below:

External reality	Interpretations	Emotions
Real-life events	Beliefs	Happiness and unhappiness in all their flavors
People	Attitudes	
Things	Thoughts	

This model illustrates that there's no causal relationship between external reality and our emotions. Instead, it's the way we *interpret* real-life events, people, and things that makes us happy or unhappy.

To illustrate this process in the simplest way, picture two men on a Saturday afternoon, sitting side by side, drinking beer in the sunshine and watching precisely the same set of events unfold. After a couple of hours, one of the men is so excited he's on his feet, pumping his fist in the air. The other is so dejected he's holding his face in his hands. Same events. Entirely opposite emotions. As supporters of rival football teams, their interpretation of what's going on couldn't be more different.

It's our interpretations, not external reality, that make us feel happy or unhappy. There really isn't a single event, person, or thing that can't be interpreted in any number of ways, each leading to a different emotional outcome. This is precisely why money, status, achievement, intimacy, sex, children, or anything else can't be reliable causes of happiness. We might find happiness in them at one moment, but when something arises to change our thoughts and interpretations, the feelings they invoke change, too.

And we're wonderfully creative in our ability to find new interpretations for any given situation. Very few people would say they aspire to be left at the altar, for example, or to receive a cancer diagnosis, but you can meet people who've experienced exactly these things who tell you it was the best thing that ever happened to them. Having recovered from the initial shock and sense of betrayal, the jilted lover explains how they have come to acknowledge deep fault lines in the relationship, previously ignored, that would have made fulfilment difficult, and how much happier they are in a subsequent relationship. The cancer patient tells you how, having been forced to confront their own mortality, they've dramatically reviewed their priorities—how they live, who they spend their time with, and what matters to them.

In each case, a major life event that could be seen as devastating has been turned into an opportunity for personal transformation. Instead of "disaster," what's happened is reinterpreted as an opportunity to lead a more authentic life.

Typical irrational beliefs

American psychologist Albert Ellis was one of the originators of the cognitive behavior movement, and is considered one of the most influential psychotherapists, along with the likes of Sigmund Freud and Carl Rogers. It was Ellis's conviction, explained in dozens of books, that most unhappiness arises from irrational thinking—a challenging notion given that depression is one of the most common reasons people go to the doctor. It's the job of a therapist to help identify the different unhelpful ways a person is interpreting reality to arrive at a feeling of depression—and then robustly challenge each one until that client recognizes why each interpretation is irrational and replaces it with a more rational one. Not so much tea and sympathy, this is a lively take-no-prisoners approach to therapy, designed to demolish the entire architecture of negative cognition that gives rise to unhappy feelings.

During his career, Ellis identified a number of widely held irrational beliefs, variations upon which were the most common causes of unhappiness. He would express these in extreme forms so that their irrationality was self-evident. They included: "It is awful and terrible when things are not the way I would very much like them to be"; "My past experience is an all-important determiner of my present behavior and because something once strongly affected my life, it should indefinitely have a similar effect"; and "I must be absolutely competent and achieving in all important respects or else I am an inadequate and worthless human being."[10]

On a moment-by-moment basis we experience real-life events through a filter of interpretations, one we're so used to that for the most part we're not even aware it's there. Irrationality, negative thinking, and unhealthy rumination are generally much easier to perceive in others than in ourselves.

We can see the unhelpful content of other people's thoughts and understand why this is taking such an emotional toll. Our own self-inflicted unhappiness, on the other hand, may not be so clearly evident to us. What's more, the process by which we perceive, think, and react emotionally is so automatic, so habitual that it happens before we know it.

Take the case of Derek, a senior executive with a tele-communications company, who has a passion for boat-building and sailing, and suddenly finds himself redundant. After working through the initial shock and anger of what happened, he may begin to focus on any number of interpretations. These could include:

- "They made me redundant because I wasn't up to the job."
- "I've lost my edge, I have few capabilities and little to offer the world."
- "I should have seen the writing on the wall, but I didn't because I'm not smart enough."
- "This is a devastating personal setback from which it will be impossible for me to recover."
- "Everyone thinks less of me because of it and I'm a disappointment to myself."
- "Even though I have some savings, they're not nearly enough to retire on. The financial impact of this is drastic."
- "I'll have to sell the boat that gives me so much pleasure, and cut down on all unnecessary expenses."

- "I don't deserve the love and support being shown to me by my family and friends."

The more these negative thoughts become ingrained in Derek's thinking, the truer they begin to seem to him. They're no longer just thoughts, they're facts. They begin to influence his behavior, and when others respond to his lack of self-confidence, this further validates his negative beliefs about himself, propelling him along the downward spiral.

But Derek could have interpreted things differently:

- "I no longer found working there fulfilling. I can't say I'll miss it at all."
- "Redundancies are common these days, almost always driven by financial imperatives."
- "I'd never have been able to justify giving up a well-paid job to start a boat-building business, but now that I'm in this position, perhaps it's a chance to try what I'm really passionate about."
- "I'm fortunate to have some savings to help me make the transition."
- "I know I can count on my family and friends for love and support."

This alternative way of framing exactly the same life event produces a very different set of feelings—and, in turn, behavior. In several years" time, when Derek's boat-building company begins to thrive, he may come to see his redundancy as the vital push he needed to move out of his comfort zone and follow his passion. Stacking the shelves of the local supermarket, meantime, doppelganger Derek is convinced that redundancy was the cruel end to life as he knew it.

Combining mindfulness with cognitive behavior training

Our focus so far has been on the *content* of thoughts, and how powerfully they affect our feelings about the external world. But there's another important element—the *process* by which our thoughts arise and trigger an emotional response.

The cognitive behavior model, skillfully applied, can give us life-changing insights into the content of our thoughts. If we suffer from depression or anxiety, for example, we can begin to understand that *what* we're thinking, the stuff of our thoughts, is leading directly to our feelings of despair or worry.

Mindfulness helps us gain control of *how* this happens: the process. When we can observe thoughts rather than automatically react to them, we start being able to manage what's going on in our minds. We create space in which we're free to choose how we respond—or not. Instead of being a victim of our thoughts, we become their observer.

The mindful state has qualities that can be very powerfully applied to transform the process by which thoughts become feelings. *Equanimity* is one such quality. Instead of events, people, or situations automatically triggering an emotional change, positive or negative, when we experience equanimity we're calm, balanced, and composed. We're less reactive. With a greater sense of ease and inner peace, we don't rush to judgement. Instead, we benefit from greater composure no matter what thoughts arise in our mind or visceral reaction in our bodies.

Non-attachment is another useful quality. The more our habit of meditation deepens, the more obvious it becomes to us that every single thought, idea, or sensation we've ever had is impermanent. It arises, abides, and passes. The more this understanding of impermanence deepens, the more it erodes our sense of attachment. We still have preferences, ambitions, likes, and dislikes, we're just not so hung up about them. Thoughts are just thoughts—not eternal truths. Instead of identifying with ideas about ourselves and others, clinging tightly to notions about the way things should be, when we discover how impermanent and insubstantial thoughts actually are, we find it much easier to let go of them. This enables us to be more spontaneous, accepting, and happier in each moment, whatever that moment happens to bring us.

Greater *awareness* is an additional quality that can empower personal transformation. Instead of our emotions being propelled by an unobserved narrative tide, perhaps coupled with bodily sensations of which we're only partly aware, we become much more conscious of every element of thought and bodily sensation. Combining heightened awareness with equanimity and non-attachment can lead to a rapid extinction of habitual responses. It can open up whole new dimensions of thought and feelings.

Avoiding the trap of habitual negativity

What happens if we're unable to do this? If we become trapped in habitual negativity?

Charles Dickens gave us the vividly etched character of Miss Havisham in *Great Expectations* as the ultimate case study. Miss Havisham discovered at twenty minutes to nine on her wedding day that her fiancé had only ever been interested in her wealth and, having successfully defrauded her, had no intention of going through with the wedding. For decades she remained inside the heavily curtained Satis House, wearing her wedding dress, emaciated and waxen, the clocks stopped at twenty to nine, the wedding cake rotting on the table.

Miss Havisham is a caricature of the self-inflicted pain of attachment—the inability or unwillingness to step away from a spiral of negative interpretations, beliefs, and emotions. Perhaps part of the reason she's such a compelling character is that there's a little of Miss Havisham in so many of us. If you've ever felt trapped in a cycle of negative thoughts and feelings, if recurring unhappiness is or has been part of your life, if you feel imprisoned from exploring and enjoying life's rich tapestry, it's almost certainly the case that all this arises not from external reality, however much you may believe this to be the case, but from your own interpretations, thoughts, and attitudes about that reality. Just as for Miss Havisham, your pain may have been unavoidable; your suffering is not.

At any moment Miss Havisham could have thrown open the curtains and let the sunshine in, wound up the clocks, cleared away the last remnants of the wedding cake, and changed into something more comfortable. At any moment we, in our own way, can do so, too. The gentle practice of mindfulness holds the key to letting go of even seemingly entrenched patterns of thought.

As we discover when we meditate, not a single thought can remain in our mind unless we lend attention to it. This revelatory finding is something we'll explore in much greater detail in Chapter 11.

The experience of mindful living

If happiness and unhappiness arise more from our thoughts about the world around us than from the world itself, and if mindfulness is the floodlight by which we illuminate the process of these thoughts coming into being, what if it were possible to live in a state of continuous mindfulness? What if, instead of investing our attention so heavily in the external circumstances of our lives, we focused more on the process and content of our thoughts? What would the outcome be then?

Fortunately for us, we don't have to look very far to find examples of people who train to live in just this way. Mindfulness is a foundation practice in Buddhism, and practitioners strive to be mindful of every action of body, speech, and mind. Given that training in mindfulness, like training in music at the Berlin Academy of Music (see Chapter 8), is a matter of putting in the hours, mindfulness practitioners who have spent the most time working on this skill will show the highest levels of competence.

Mindfulness is a relatively new concept in the West, so we need to look to the East for examples of people who meet this criterion. What we find is that the most accomplished meditators, lamas, yogis, and gurus, whatever their tradition, share a number of qualities. Among these are a lightness of being and a sense of ease, even playfulness. Although they may keep fairly strict routines, they respond spontaneously, rather than predictably, to events that arise—in their company you have the sense that anything may or can happen.

An important focus of their attention, and lives, tends to be the well-being of others. Whether they engage in solitary meditation retreats, teach in ashrams, or live in the community, they show a developed empathy for other beings, human and animal. This manifests itself in different ways among different practitioners—some living quietly but compassionately in the background, others becoming widely known and much loved for their ability to connect from the heart.

Long-term meditators and mindfulness practitioners tend to have a positive outlook on life no matter what happens. They relish life's pleasures, whether that involves simple meals and daily interactions or whatever exotic holidays and luxuries they may enjoy. Hardships and challenges don't overly preoccupy them—they have a more panoramic outlook in which mundane frustrations are kept in perspective. Not even death itself holds particular fear, their first-hand experience of the nature of mind giving them an understanding of the continuity of consciousness beyond death.

An engagement with the natural world is usually of keen interest to long-term meditators, as is an enduring interest in all aspects of spirituality—though not necessarily the forms and rituals of organized religion.

Wealth and possessions are of relatively low priority. While not wishing to become a burden on society, long-term meditators value surplus wealth mainly for the benefit it may provide to others. The idea that happiness might depend on owning a particular house, car, or investment portfolio would simply make a long-term meditator laugh, as would any suggestion that a particular relationship, achievement, or other external condition has any significance at all beyond whatever we choose to give it.

Of primary importance is mind itself. That is the source of all happiness and unhappiness—which begs the question: what *is* mind?

10

What is mind?

There are two ways to be fooled. One is
to believe what isn't true; the other is to
refuse to believe what is true.

SØREN KIERKEGAARD[1]

One of life's greatest paradoxes is that even though our entire experience of reality depends on our mind, most of us seldom stop to ask what mind actually is. Everything we perceive, think, and feel arises because of our mind. We've felt every frustration, triumph, misery, or joy only with mind's participation. It's actually impossible to sense, connect, and respond to anything without the involvement of mind. Mind is the ever-present continuum flowing through our lives from our first moment of consciousness until our last. And mindfulness profoundly influences our health and happiness.

That being the case, wouldn't it be useful to have a good working knowledge of what mind actually is? There are reasons why some people may feel they can't answer this question. Those with a religious background may believe that probing too deeply into the nature of mind is trespassing onto church ground. If mind is bound up with the soul, then "What is mind?" becomes a religious question, a matter of faith rather than something to which there is a definitive answer.

Other people may think this question is quite properly the preserve of psychiatrists, neuroscientists, and other highly educated experts whose knowledge of brain functioning gives them an understanding greatly superior to anything that people without such an education can possibly hope to achieve. "What is mind?" may be a good question, but according to this view, unless you have the right postgraduate degree, you'll be unable to answer it.

Other people still may simply be overwhelmed by the question. The subject may seem too vast, complex, or overwhelming. Where do you begin?

In this chapter I'd like to explain what mind is—not according to any belief system, hypothesis, or theory, but in a way you can experience directly for yourself. Exploring your own mind may very well be the most valuable, surprising, and liberating undertaking of your life.

Before getting there, it's useful to explore how conventional ideas about mind have evolved, and why we're privileged to be living in an era when an amazing convergence is taking place—between scientists and meditators, East and West, ancient and contemporary, outer and inner.

Mind as soul and the mind–body duality

Despite the primacy of mind, in the West the question "What is mind?" has been more or less ignored until quite recently. From the time of Pythagoras, early scientific and philosophical inquiry focused on the external world. During the Renaissance era, scientists such as Copernicus, Kepler, and Galileo believed the universe was a celestial machine ruled by immutable mathematical principles, and that it was the job of science to discover what those principles were. They believed the entire cosmos was separate from human experience and independent of human perception.

There was a powerful reason why early scientists didn't concern themselves with questions about the mind: it was seen as indistinguishable from the soul. Cognition, emotion, and consciousness were all bound up with the soul, an entity with no relation to material reality. So distinct was the soul—and the mind with it—from matter that it was seen as completely separate from even the body.

René Descartes, sometimes referred to as the father of modern philosophy, summed up this view in his book *Discourse on the Method*, published in 1637, when he explained the reasoning behind his famous dictum "I think therefore I am":

From this I knew I was a substance whose whole essence or nature is solely to think, and which does not require any place, or depend on any material thing, in order to exist. Accordingly this "I"—that is, the soul by which I am what I am—is entirely distinct from the body, and indeed is easier to know than the body, and would not fail to be whatever it is, even if the body did not exist.[2]

The problems with mind-body duality

Had Descartes had the benefit of attending a weekly yoga class, it's highly unlikely he would ever have come up with a line such as "I think therefore I am." As practitioners of mindfulness, yoga students come to understand *asmita*, the mechanism that gives rise to the feeling of an "I."

When we reflect on our inner monologue, it turns out that the vast majority of our thoughts are about ourselves. "Me," "myself," and "I" are the focus of our ongoing narrative each day. So automatic is this process that, without even realizing what we're doing, we weave "self" into whatever is happening at the time.

As Michael Stone explains in *The Inner Tradition of Yoga*, let's say we adopt a yoga pose and experience pain in the knee. In our inner narrative, we don't say, "There's pain in the knee." Instead we say, "There's a pain in *my* knee":

> *In this instinctual moment, an "I" is born that has inserted itself into the phenomenon of pain, but was not initially built into the sensation. In other words, the feeling of pain in "my" knee is an addition to what is unfolding. This is the beginning of duality, because through aversion, a sense of self is created that separates the experience from the one who is experiencing.[3]*

Descartes need not even have put himself through the ordeal of performing sun salutations. Had he simply allowed his mind to settle into its natural state, he would have observed that thoughts arise quite naturally. They just happen. They require no active agent—no me, myself, or I. In fact, they arise *despite* the wishes of the I. Some meditation teachers like to tease their students by asking how a session was for them. If a student says their meditation was disrupted by thoughts, the teacher asks: "Did you not choose to have those thoughts?" When the student shakes their head, the teacher says: "If you didn't cause the thoughts to arise, then who did?"

"Thoughts arise" admittedly doesn't pack quite the same punch as "I think therefore I am," but one can but contemplate the alternative course western philosophy might have taken had Descartes opted for the former rather than the latter.

There's a separate, quite obvious problem with Descartes's famous dualism: the division of mind and body into two "entirely distinct" entities. If it really was the case that whatever happened in our mind was completely independent of our bodies, then thoughts would have no physical effect and physical pain would similarly have no impact on mental equilibrium. But it's obvious that neither of these things is true.

According to Descartes's definition, there's no reason why a thought should cause the blood vessels in our cheeks to dilate suddenly, but that's exactly what happens when we blush. The opposite happens to some people when they get a shock. Why would you go "white as a sheet" if the content of your thoughts was entirely dislocated from your body? Perhaps the most important evidence for the non-duality of body and mind is sexual arousal. There was no need for Mr. Wilkins to explain to his classroom of testosterone-charged teenage boys that sexual arousal can be triggered by erotic thought alone. We had all of us made that discovery already.

Conversely, the idea that our mental equanimity is entirely unaffected by what happens to our body seems an incredible suggestion to make: a single mosquito bite is sometimes all it takes to disturb our peace of mind.

Far from being "entirely distinct," body and mind are fully integrated within the same systemic whole.

Mind as brain

The fact that the mind–soul was the preserve of religious mystery goes some way to explaining why this subject wasn't a focus of scientific scrutiny. But as the hold of the church began to weaken, scientists shifted their stance from seeking to illuminate the perfection of God's creation to a more God-neutral position. This shift is compellingly illustrated in the famous encounter between Napoleon and Pierre-Simon Laplace, a brilliant mathematical astronomer, in the early 1800s. History tells us that Laplace delivered a polished exposition of the movement of the earth and planets according to the laws of physics. The French emperor paid close attention—one imagines with one hand tucked into his waistcoat, the other nursing a balloon snifter of cognac. After Laplace had finished his explanation, Napoleon asked why he'd made no mention of the creator. Laplace is said to have replied, "I have no need for that hypothesis."

Over a period of time, scientists came to explain the workings of the physical world without the need to refer to any non-material forces or energies. At a universal level the idea of a supernatural being standing outside creation became unnecessary, and correspondingly, at a human level, the notion of a soul became redundant, too. Scientists believed they could explain the working of human beings without having to refer to anything that wasn't strictly physical. According to this view, only matter is real. The mind is the brain. Mental activity equals brain activity.

You might say that at this point scientists threw out the baby of the mind along with the metaphysical bathwater. Scientific materialism grew to become not so much the consensus opinion as the dogmatic ideology of science for most of the past two-hundred years. Curiously, although the doctrine of materialism isn't to be found on any school curriculum, it's assumed in questions such as "What is the biological basis of consciousness?" which appeared as recently as 2005 when the journal *Science* published a special anniversary edition featuring 125 questions scientists had so far failed to answer.[4]

The idea that consciousness may not be adequately described in biological or material terms was simply seen as unscientific, anti-scientific, or taboo.

The problems with materialism

This "mind as brain" view is as flawed as Descartes's disembodied soul.

The most obvious problem is the lack of an explanation as to how consciousness can arise from matter. Some scientists adopted the denial strategy, saying that mind and consciousness didn't actually exist. In 1953, the American behaviorist B.F. Skinner went as far as to say that they were "invented for the sole purpose of providing spurious explanations . . . Since mental or psychic events are asserted to lack the dimensions of physical science, we have an additional reason for rejecting them."[5]

Others, such as Francis Crick, the co-discoverer of DNA, explained that consciousness was simply the subjective experience of brain activity: " 'You,' your joys and your sorrows, your memories and your ambitions, your sense of personal identity and free will, are in fact no more than the behavior of a vast assembly of nerve cells and their associated molecules . . ."[6]

What materialists failed to explain was how cells, molecules, and atoms could give rise to consciousness when they have no consciousness-creating properties. Scientists wishing to account for this problem would invoke "complexity" as the reason. Create a complex enough network of neurons and—whoosh!—consciousness arises. But in the words of B. Alan Wallace:

no matter how complex this network of cells might be, it strikes me as mystical thinking to imagine that something as

radically different as an emotion or a dream could emerge
from neurons. We could just as easily believe in the emer-
gence of a genie from a magic lamp.[7]

The hold of reductionist materialism, still strong today, is especially puzzling when you consider that it fails to explain some of the most basic aspects of mental activity. Take memory. Recall ability is an assumed part of our moment-to-moment consciousness. If mind really is brain alone, then memories must be physically stored somewhere in the brain. But attempts to find memory traces have been unsuccessful despite billions of dollars spent on decades of research.

In the early twentieth century, psychologist Karl Lashley carried out a gruesome series of experiments in which he destroyed different parts of rats" brains in an attempt to locate the center of memory. To his surprise, he found he could burn out even large amounts of brain tissue and the rats would still remember how to find their way to food. From this emerged his theory of "equipotentiality"—if certain parts of the brain were damaged, other parts would take on their role.

Exactly how memories might be physically stored in brain cells is a particular conundrum given that these cells, like all others in our body, are subject to ongoing death and replacement. How are memories handed on from one cell to another? Or leap from destroyed brain cells to cells that were intact, in the case of the rats who had parts of their brains destroyed?

The loss of memory due to brain injury or the ravages of Alzheimer's disease is sometimes offered as evidence that memory resides in the affected areas. If that were the case, then other people lacking these same parts of the brain would be similarly affected. But British neurologist John Lorber, who scanned the brains of more than 600 people, discovered that the cranial cavity of about 10 percent of these was more than 95 percent filled with cerebrospinal fluid. In other words, they had tiny brains. While some individuals were retarded, others were mentally normal and several performed extremely well in IQ tests. One individual with a first-class degree in mathematics and an IQ of 126 had a brain only 5 percent of the normal size. This led Lorber to ask a provocative question: is the brain really necessary for higher-level thinking?

Consciousness experiences when the brain stops working

If the fundamental question of where memory is stored cannot be answered, there's little need to search for further shortcomings in the reductionist model, although it is worth looking at experiences of consciousness when the brain becomes inactive. Near-death experiences (NDEs) are one example of this.

While stories of NDEs have always been with us, in the past thirty years or so as resuscitation techniques have become significantly more effective, especially following cardiac arrests, reports of NDEs have become more widespread. The sheer volume of cases has given rise to significant research by eminent medical specialists and researchers such as Raymond Moody, Kenneth Ring, Michael Sabom, and Bruce Greyson. In separate and thorough bodies of work they have categorized typical elements of NDEs. These and many other aspects of NDEs are explored in some detail in *Conciousness Beyond Life* by Dr. Pim van Lommel.[8] While there's no such thing as a standard NDE, people may experience one or more of the following: an out-of-body experience where they see themselves from above or outside their body; a strong awareness of being dead; an overwhelming feeling of peace, joy, and bliss; moving through a dark tunnel; the perception of an extremely bright, non-blinding light that permeates everything; a panoramic life review; communicating with deceased people; and so on.

Reviewing the implications of NDE studies in an article in the *Journal of Near-Death Studies*, Dr. Penny

Sartori concluded: "The fact that clear, lucid experiences were reported during a time when the brain was devoid of activity . . . does not sit easily with current scientific belief."[9]

NDEs are not the only medically related phenomenon that conflicts with the material model. Arguably even more striking are patients who experience lucid consciousness while in a coma. In such cases, their brains are subject to multiple scans. Medical evidence may demonstrate that the brain has ceased to function. And yet people who experience comas sometimes emerge reporting the most vivid moments of consciousness of their lives.

One such coma patient was Dr. Eben Alexander, who became comatose for seven days in November 2008 after contracting a severe brain infection. Dr. Alexander was a particularly interesting case because after completing a fellowship in cerebrovascular neurosurgery in the United Kingdom, he spent fifteen years at Harvard Medical School as an associate professor of surgery with a specialization in neurosurgery. Dr. Alexander explains his view of consciousness before his coma: "the brain is the machine that produces consciousness . . . When the machine breaks down, consciousness stops . . . Pull the plug and the TV goes dead . . . so I would have told you before my own brain crashed."[10]

In his book *Proof of Heaven*, Dr. Alexander recalls the life-changing and transcendent consciousness events he experienced while in a coma. He also freely admits he would have denied the possibility of what had happened to him had he not experienced it himself:

> Like many other scientific skeptics, I refused to even review the data relevant to the questions concerning these phenomena. I prejudiced the data, and those providing it, because my limited perspective failed to provide the foggiest notion of how such things might actually happen. Those who assert that there is no evidence for phenomena indicative of extended consciousness, in spite of overwhelming evidence to the contrary, are willfully ignorant. They believe they know the truth without needing to look at the facts.[11]

Dr. Alexander's book contains an intriguing appendix in which he explores nine separate neuroscientific hypotheses that might explain his experience in biological terms. You need to be a neuroscientist to understand some of them, but what's important is that, as he himself concludes, they all fail to account for what happened. No matter what elaborate or unlikely explanations are offered, the basic premise that mind and brain are the same thing simply can't be sustained.

And then came relativity
and quantum physics

Albert Michelson, winner of the Nobel Prize for Physics, made a significant announcement in 1894:

> *The more important fundamental laws and facts of physical science have all been discovered, and these are now so firmly established that the possibility of their ever being supplanted in consequence of new discoveries is exceedingly remote . . . Our future discoveries must be looked for in the sixth place of decimals.*[12]

This turned out to be not only an overconfident assertion, but a prediction that couldn't have been more wrong. Within twenty years, Einstein had published his general and special theories of relativity, which changed much, and physicists such as Werner Heisenberg, Erwin Schrödinger, and Niels Bohr went on to develop quantum theory. So fundamentally different was the quantum science view of reality, that Bohr summed it up in the following words: "Those who are not shocked when they first come across quantum theory cannot possibly have understood it."[13]

With relativity, out went the comfortably predictable Newtonian foundation of the universe in which an objective observer could describe physical activity, from the grand vision of rotating planets in the celestial machine to the neat subdivisions of organs into cells, cells into molecules, and molecules into atoms. And while relativity shattered long-held conceptions of time and space, quantum theory finished off the notion that it's even possible for people to be objective agents of observation. Instead, quantum physics threw open the doors to a more exciting reality that might be summarized according to the following three principles:

1 Matter is energy.

2 Matter/energy is interconnected.

3 Subject and object are one.

Matter is energy

At the most fundamental level, quantum science dismissed the idea that physical matter is solid. Instead, everything is both particle and wave, or particle and energy. Subatomic particles aren't solid little billiard balls that can be tidily defined, but instead are like vibrating packets of energy. Their particle-like properties confine them to particular space. At the same time their wave-like properties are dramatically more diffuse, spreading them out over both space and time. Matter and energy are not two separate entities but different expressions of the same reality, the quantitative and qualitative, the physical and psychical. As Austrian physicist Erwin Schrödinger explained, everything—anything at all—is at the same time particle and field. In the same way, special relativity revealed in the world's most famous equation—$E = mc^2$—that matter and energy are one and the same.

The implications of this for the way we understand the body, including the brain, are far-reaching. We're not flesh and blood alone, but also fields of energy. Relativity and quantum science tell us that the bodily form we generally experience ourselves as being is but one dimension of what we are.

···············*Matter/energy is interconnected*···············

At a subatomic level, scientists also discovered the concept of non-locality. Far from the predictability of classic physics, this consequence of quantum entanglement is the ability of quantum particles to influence each other over any distance even when no exchange of energy takes place between them. It appears that once these particles/waves have been in contact, they retain a connection, an ability to influence each other, no matter how far they may be separated.

In the words of Sir James Jeans, who in the 1940s coined the phrase "new physics" to describe the shift from the principles of the mechanical age:

We may picture the world of reality as a deep-flowing stream; the world of appearance is its surface, below which we cannot see. Events deep down in the stream throw up bubbles and eddies on the surface of the stream. These are the transfers of energy and radiation of our common life, which affect our senses and so activate our minds; below these lie deep waters.[14]

Non-locality refers not only to space, but also to time. This is the context of Einstein's famous quote, a condensed version of which is much loved by fridge-magnet manufacturers around the world: "People like us, who believe in physics, know that the distinction between past, present, and future is only a stubborn, persistent illusion."[15]

Subject and object are one

Another profound change brought about by both relativity and quantum physics is that no distinction can be drawn between the observer and the observed. Out went the old, classical notion that scientists can be objective witnesses to activities that occur independently of their observation. Instead, the state of all possibilities of any quantum phenomenon is now known to collapse into just one entity as soon as it's observed or quantified.

There's no such thing as an "objective" observer. Observation is, in reality, a participatory activity. The act of observing forces phenomena into a fixed state. It's our own consciousness that makes things appear to us the way they do. Things don't and can't exist independently of our minds. Every moment of every day, in a very literal way, we're creating our own reality.

Take the everyday example of the woman on her way to work one grey morning. Heading towards the office, she passes a coffee shop and smells the delicious aroma of roasted coffee beans. She decides to cheer herself up with a cappuccino. Contemporary physicists will confirm that there are no such things as grey molecules in the sky or anywhere else. Photons are emitted by molecules, but photons are comprised of energy, not color. Photons strike the retina and set off a complex sequence of processes in the visual cortex, which possesses no "grey zone" and is heavily dependent on inputs from other parts of the brain associated with memory. As a result of this process, which no one can explain, the woman sees "grey." The grey isn't outside her, it's not in her brain, nor does it exist anywhere in between.

Ditto the aroma of coffee.

Color, scent, and sounds, to use just a few examples of "qualia" (subjective conscious experiences), have no material existence. They do not reside in atoms or molecules. They have no weight. Although they are phenomena of which we are constantly aware and on which we shape our lives, the simple truth is that they don't exist apart from us.

Erwin Schrödinger put this plainly when he said, "Subject and object are only one. The barrier between them cannot be said to have broken down as a result of recent experience in the physical sciences, for this barrier does not exist."[16]

Mind as a flow of energy

Where does this leave us in our understanding of mind? Having moved from the Renaissance idea of mind as soul, through the materialist notion of mind as brain, scientists are now deepening their understanding of mind as a flow of energy, capable of consciousness and cognition.

This explanation shares certain elements of the previous paradigms, while dealing with their more evident flaws. Like Descartes's soul, the energy model is not synonymous with the body or, more specifically, the brain. Particle can still be labeled "particle." Wave can be called "wave." But they *are* two dimensions of the same reality. We don't tie ourselves up in dualistic knots trying to account for how the mind and body can be separate yet be affected by each other. The one is an expression of the other.

Materialists, meanwhile, were correct to identify brain functioning as central to mental activity, but the energy model sees the role of the brain not so much as command central as more akin to a receiver, like a TV set, an important nexus between energy and matter. Removing different components from a TV set may have a variety of impacts on reception. Damage to one circuit may deprive us of color. A different fault may cause us to lose sound. But these specific problems relate only to that particular TV set. Even a completely damaged TV, incapable of functioning, doesn't equal the end of broadcasting—only a problem with that particular receiver. The idea that the broadcast continues despite the malfunctioning of the receiver is precisely the point made by neurosurgeon Dr. Eben Alexander in *Proof of Heaven*, and Dr. Pim van Lommel in *Consciousness Beyond Life*.

The notion of the brain having an energetic dimension has long been an accepted part of conventional medicine—it's the basis of electroencephalographs (EEGs), which are widely used in medicine to monitor brain activity (of particular benefit in the diagnosis of conditions such as epilepsy), in measuring the depth of anesthesia, and in identifying brain activity in comatose patients. Consciousness and energy are, to some extent, already seen as synonymous.

Non-locality implies connections through time and space, reflecting the subjective nature of our thoughts, which range with apparent randomness and freedom to events and places far distant. And in the quantum field, in which any number of potentialities may arise, those that do are a construct of mind as much as they are a reflection of what's "out there." Reality is ours alone.

This model of mind is fascinating for many reasons, not least among them that western science has brought us to much the same destination as eastern contemplative traditions.

······ *Convergence in eastern and western thought* ······

In his introduction to *Einstein and Buddha*, meditation teacher and broadcaster Wes Nisker likens the earth to the two hemispheres of the brain. The West represents the left hemisphere, its most gifted thinkers searching for the truth about reality by looking outward, deconstructing, and analyzing the material universe, using the deductive powers of reasoning. The East represents the right hemisphere, its wisest people turning their attention inward, seeking truth in the nature of consciousness, the origin of mental events, and the relationship between body and mind. Mind was the starting point, because experience is only possible through consciousness. You might say that while the East has traditionally been holistic, the West is more focused on identifying distinctions.

Nisker observes:

In our time, modern communications and travel have served as a corpus callosum, connecting the two hemispheres and revealing an astonishing agreement about the laws of nature and the structure of deep reality. Taken together, we now have what might be called "the full-brain approach."[17]

The method of enquiry in East and West has been much the same. Whether scrutinizing the movement of the planets or the activity of the mind, investigators have had to spend many thousands of hours observing what appears, developing explanations to account for it, and having their accounts replicated, challenged, or accepted by others.

Common languages evolved to describe the phenomena. Discoveries are reported, analyzed, and refined. The sages of the East, like the scientists of the West, have followed clearly prescribed and rigorous discipline. In their studies, both have honored the notion of remaining nonjudgemental about what they observe.

The Buddhist definition of mind

In the East, the result of this inquiry into the nature of the mind may be summed up in the Buddhist definition of the mind: "A formless continuum of clarity and cognition."[18] While simply expressed, this definition has profound implications.

A formless continuum . . .

The word "formless" in this definition means that mind is not inherently matter. It is boundless and has no beginning or end. There are no material limits to our subjective experience of our mind. In fact, the very notion of mind having boundaries may be described as a "category mistake"— that is, attributing to it qualities it can't possibly possess because those qualities belong to a different category of phenomenon.

"Continuum" points to the continuity in our experience of mind, with one mind moment constantly following another, like the flow of a river. Mind is not static—it has an energetic, dynamic quality. "Continuum" describes the way that each mind moment arises as a result of a previous mind moment, not in a linear way—any glimpse of one's own mind will soon establish that—but as an effect of a previously created cause.

In the last chapter we looked at how mindfulness, coupled with cognitive behavior training, can lead to the rapid extinction of negative habits and feelings. Both the arising and ending of these negative habits is only possible because mind is a continuum. While western psychology has been mostly preoccupied with eliminating dysfunctional behavior, Buddhists are more interested in the ultimate possible upside of this continuum: if we can self-consciously shift the direction of its trajectory, why aim for anything less than enlightenment itself—or at least "self-actualization," the objective proposed by psychologist Abraham Maslow?

You could say that the quantum physics concepts of non-locality and energy are embraced in the Buddhist definition of a "formless continuum": our minds can and do roam freely through time and space.

While the energetic field that is our mind is focused around our bodies during life, it won't always be so. Death is certain. But the end of the TV set isn't the end of the broadcast. Energy cannot be created or destroyed, but it is capable of change. The formless continuum of mind goes on, and the Buddhist view is that cause and effect, observable within the formless continuum of mind during this lifetime, continues from one lifetime to the next.

"Clarity" points to the ultimate nature of mind, a quality capable of reflecting, perceiving, and experiencing all form. Buddhist teachers use several different analogies to illustrate clarity of mind. The sky is one such metaphor, with every thought like a cloud that passes through it. No matter whether it's a happy, fluffy cloud that briskly scoots from one horizon to the other, or an overcast pall that seems to hang around interminably, there comes a time when every cloud has gone from the sky. And when it does it leaves no residue, no trace.

A mirror is another favorite metaphor. It dispassionately reflects whatever arises, but is in no way affected by what appears. No matter how distressing a trauma, how chronic a habit, how ecstatic an encounter, there comes a point when it's no longer present. Mind returns to primordial, pristine clarity.

This concept of mind as naturally clear and free of obscuration is quite different from religious convictions about human nature being sinful and separated from love or other expressions of divinity. According to the Buddhist definition, beliefs and convictions, like other mental activity, are temporary and changeable. This is not to diminish their importance in the way they color our experience of reality for a period of time. It's rather a way of saying we shouldn't confuse the clouds for the sky, our thoughts for the mind. They arise, abide, and pass. The more we engage with and empower them, the longer they abide. But they have no meaning or permanence without our involvement. Rather than paying undue attention to such ephemera, what's important is to focus on what actually endures—the clarity of mind.

"Clarity," in everyday usage, has connotations of neutrality, of absence, but in the context of mind, the experience of clarity is not a tedious void of sensory deprivation. On the contrary, words often used to describe it include "radiant," "luminous," and even "blissful."

. . . *and cognition*

"Cognition" is the ability to perceive and understand. The word encompasses all elements of mental activity, including our capacity to sense, interpret, think, remember, plan, visualize, and so on.

In Buddhism as in quantum physics there is, importantly, no suggestion of an independent world out there with which a person engages. The reason no person, object, or situation can be a reliable cause of happiness—as explored in the last chapter—is that it has no inherent qualities that can give rise to happiness. Instead, each of us projects happiness-giving characteristics onto people and phenomena in the outside world. Or not.

We already have some understanding of this. Adages such as "One man's meat is another man's poison" reflect our awareness of the subjectivity of experience. The Buddhist view that nothing can exist independently, separately, or inherently takes this subjectivity to its ultimate conclusion.

Buddha himself summarized this when he said simply, "The objective world rises from the mind itself."[19] Two and a half millennia later, quantum physicist Erwin Schrödinger arrived at precisely the same conclusion: "Every man's world picture is and always remains a construct of his mind and cannot be proved to have any other existence."[20]

Change your mind, change your reality

The value of this understanding of mind is not simply to improve our mental functioning—it is to transform our reality. When we change our mind, we change our world. From this perspective, trying to get everything in the outside world into a state that will deliver happiness is a strategy guaranteed to fail because it's based on the false premise that things out there are inherently real. On the other hand, abiding in the true nature of our own mind, a nature that's radiant and blissful, is a more reliable source of contentment, because it's based on an accurate experience of reality.

As Buddhist monk, teacher, and author Matthieu Ricard explains in *The Quantum and the Lotus*, "For Buddhism, there has never been a solid reality with an intrinsic existence. Enlightenment simply consists in awakening from a dream of ignorance that attributes this intrinsic reality to objects."[21]

The understanding of mind and reality shared by Buddhism and quantum physics is radical and thought-provoking, and can take us in a number of intriguing philosophical directions. But its true value lies in its application. Buddhism has always been more concerned with practical use than with theoretical abstractions, however fascinating.

So, how do we experience this formless continuum of clarity and cognition? And what happens to reality when we do?

11

How to meditate on your own mind

No man ever steps in the same river twice;
For it is not the same river, and he is not the
same man.

HERACLITUS

To experience the nature of our own mind for ourselves by meditating on it, the instructions are simple. We begin by adopting the physical and psychological postures already explained in Chapter 3 of this book.

Next, we undertake a breath-based meditation for some time to help settle the mind. Whether you choose the breath-counting or nine-cycle method is up to you. Similarly, the length of time you focus on your breath is a matter of personal judgment and your current state of mind. If your mind is very agitated, it may take longer to settle. If it's already as smooth as the surface of a tranquil lake, a shorter time is needed. As before, use mindfulness and awareness to sustain attention on the breath.

Having settled your mind to some extent, now change the object of meditation from your breath to mind itself. Don't worry if this takes some time to get used to. It may very well be the first time you've tried to find your own mind. (For a step-by-step summary of how to meditate on mind, see the end of this chapter.)

While the breath is known as a "gross" object of meditation in that it's easy to find, the mind is a "subtle" object and may prove elusive. You may find yourself staring into your closed eyelids as if physically looking for the mind. Or caught up in narrative analysis about trying to find the mind.

The first few times I tried this meditation I found it very irritating indeed. My mind was so filled with gross agitation I felt I had been set an impossible task. The observation that some of my fellow meditators clearly looked forward to the practice only irked me the more. But somehow, over the weeks, months, and years, things turned around. "Mind watching mind" became one of *my* favorites! I mention this especially for those readers whose initial experience is the same as mine was. Don't dismiss the practice, and don't give up. Put it to one side if you like until you build up your concentration muscles, but come back to it.

There are many people, unlike me, who take to this meditation immediately. I hope you're one of them! I know of no more direct way of coming home to yourself than through this practice.

Just as when you're doing a breathing meditation, the first thing you'll probably observe when you try to focus on your mind is agitation. For a few moments you may experience a sense of spaciousness and then, before you know it, up pops a thought.

When we do a breathing meditation and our focus is, say, on the sensation of the breath at the tip of our nostrils, if a thought arises it's a distraction. But when we practice "mind watching mind" meditation the good news is that because thoughts are a part of mind, they're part of the object of meditation. This may be likened to sitting on a bench overlooking a beach and watching the sea. If you watch waves arise from the water, form a crest, then break onto the beach, you're still watching the sea. The waves are not somehow separate entities from the sea. They consist of the same stuff. For a few moments they may emerge with certain identifiable elements, but then they return from whence they came, indistinguishable from the rest of the ocean.

The same relationship exists between mind and thoughts. Every thought we've ever had arises from mind, abides for a period, and then dissolves back into mind. In the words of the Dalai Lama:

> *Just as waves disappear into water because they are of the nature of water, likewise thoughts naturally subside since they are of the nature of mind. They do not go beyond having a nature of mere clarity and awareness. Therefore when we scrutinize the nature of thoughts, we see that they automatically dissolve. Thus we come to the foundation of thought—mere clarity and awareness itself.*[1]

Meditation teachers often like to ask "Where do thoughts come from? Where do they go?" Rather than answer these questions conceptually, we're invited to observe our minds, to see for ourselves how thoughts arise, abide, and dissolve.

Although in this meditation there's no problem with observing any thought that arises in our mind as merely a thought, our challenge is to restrict ourselves to this alone: our natural tendency is to do the opposite and engage with whatever thought we have. No sooner have we finished with that particular thought—in fact, we may still be very much engaged with it—than some other sensation, stimulus, or concept catches our attention, and we're away thinking about that. B. Alan

Wallace amusingly labels this "obsessive-compulsive delusional disorder" (OCDD):

> Obsessive thoughts appear continuously, like water dripping from a leaky faucet. Thoughts arise even when there is nothing in particular to think about, and compulsive grasping compounds the problem. Absorbed by our thoughts, we identify them as being true and real, and in so doing we become delusional, very much as if we had fallen into a nonlucid dream. If we weren't so habituated to this bizarre condition, we would be crying out for help![2]

Acknowledge, accept, let go

How do we deal with the endless arising of thoughts in our mind? The time-honored technique is to apply a simple three-step process: acknowledge, accept, let go.

Acknowledgement means we don't ignore thoughts or try to suppress them. It's futile trying to do so, because it's natural for thoughts to arise. Beating ourselves up because this happens isn't helpful. It also shows we don't understand that thoughts are actually of the same nature as mind—an understanding that makes more sense non-conceptually (see below) and therefore takes time to achieve.

Accepting a thought as merely a thought is better. This reflects the nonjudgmental element of mindfulness. We're not marking our meditation performance down because thoughts keep arising. Nonjudgment is a more skillful method that embodies the insight attributed to psychologist Carl Jung: "What you resist, persists." The success with which we can see a thought as merely a thought is not accomplished by trying harder but, counterintuitively, by relaxing more deeply while maintaining our keen awareness.

When we *let go* of a thought we're choosing not to engage with it. In so doing, we're developing an enormously important capability, one that will strengthen over time. "Letting go" is the opposite of what we usually do when we have a thought, which is to engage with it. This behavior can be likened to that of a passenger on the busy rail network of a major city, where the platform is the point of neutral observation and every thought is like a train. Our usual modus operandi with our thoughts is to jump on the first train that shows up, no matter where it's headed. As soon as it comes to a stop, we jump out and, seeing another train across the platform, rush to jump onto that one. The trains may take us in circles. We may repeatedly take the same train, even though we don't want to be on it. Because we suffer from OCDD we just can't help ourselves. Along comes a train—and with a hop, skip, and a jump, we're on it!

When we acknowledge, accept, and let go, we're like the passenger on the platform who's quite willing to watch a train arrive, open its doors, close them again, and pull out, without feeling the need to get on board. As we behave this way over time, fewer trains tend to show up.

Remember that thoughts can't survive without our attention

When we begin to observe our own minds, we make all kinds of unexpected discoveries and this is often among the first of them: no thought can survive without our attention. Every thought we've ever had has gone. No matter how debilitating the thought or how triumphant, how profound or how superficial, like every other thought it has arisen, remained for a while and passed.

There's nothing permanent about our thoughts, and they'll only endure for any time at all if we give them our attention. The more we feed them, the longer they stay and the likelier it is that they'll return.

We can observe this time and again. If a thought arises and we acknowledge and accept it only as a thought, it disappears. We might use the analogy of thoughts being like small creatures in the back of a cave when we shine the powerful flashlight of our attention into the darkness. With barely a scuttle of tiny feet, they've disappeared. We find that, far from us being at the mercy of our thoughts, *they* need *us* to survive. We're not their victims but their life support.

Feelings of well-being and happiness will recur if we choose only to engage with the thoughts that give rise to them, such as thoughts of gratitude, love, and compassion. Conversely, a sense of depression, stress, or anxiety will be fueled if we engage with thoughts of being a victim or of feeling under pressure or threat.

Making this discovery can be immensely liberating. Many people have a vague, unspoken idea of the mind as being somehow fixed and beyond our ken. Thoughts just arise out of the unknowable black box, and we're stuck with them and how they make us feel. We're condemned to be permanently haunted by every hurt of the past, stuck with every traumatic memory. The weight of every failure is layered on each disappointment that preceded it. The painful truths we know about ourselves become permanent disfigurements in the concretized landscape of our minds.

Some people feel that in some way they *are* their thoughts, that their minds are some kind of invisible aggregate of every thought, feeling, memory, and belief they have—a sort of mental asset list. Fortunately, this notion of mind is just plain wrong. We can prove this by observing our own minds for ourselves.

We find that, far from being concretized, mind is clear. Instead of being fixed, mind has flow.

None of this is to trivialize whatever suffering or horror we may have had to endure. It's entirely natural for us to dwell on personal loss, injustice, and difficulties, as well as to experience the negative emotions that follow as a result. But the transience of thoughts gives us hope, a means of unlocking the door so that instead of remaining imprisoned by suffering, in time we can open the door of our unwittingly self-created prison cell and move on.

Ask: "Where did that thought come from?"

One tip I have found helpful with this practice is to ask when a thought arises, "Where did that thought come from?" This is a spatial question. We're not seeking some neurobiological explanation, we're asking, quite literally, *where* it came from. Left or right? Front or back? Up or down?

It's a useful question because it helps us see thoughts as only thoughts. We sit there, like an air traffic controller, just waiting, practically begging, for a thought to arise so we can identify its trajectory. We have no interest in whether it's Jet Blue or Delta, Airbus or Boeing. We have no interest at all in the content of the thought. We just want to pin down where it's coming from. That sense of disregard for content is generally quite new for us. It helps us cultivate an objectivity towards thoughts that counters our usual thought-hugging impulse to engage with everything that pops into our mind.

After a while, if we can maintain an objective stance towards our thoughts, we find that they arise less frequently. Even if our mind is very agitated, with practice we find that the gaps between the ending of one thought and the arising of another become longer. We're able to calm the mind, a process sometimes known by the Sanskrit term *shamatha*.

Focus on the background as well as the foreground

Another idea you may like to try out is taking a wide-angle perspective instead of focusing on the foreground of mental activity. In this instance, you might think of your thoughts as coming onto the stage of a theatre or the center court of an arena—the place where it's all happening. Well, don't fix your attention there, or you'll quite naturally find yourself drawn into whatever drama is playing out. Instead, retain a more panoramic perspective, foreground and background. This has the effect of de-emphasizing the activity in the foreground. When it happens it's of less compelling interest because it's not the only place we're "looking." We're retaining a much wider perspective.

This approach is somewhat akin to that of bodyguards who protect VIPs such as the president of the United States. They're usually standing right beside their VIP, but unlike everyone else they're never looking at the center of attention. They're always scanning the bigger picture as they search for potential threats to the VIP's security.

In your encounter with the boundless clarity of your own mind, keep your inner gaze on the big picture, the wide angle, the broadest possible perspective.

Nonconceptual versus conceptual experiences of mind

You may not be surprised to know that my favorite illustration of conceptual versus nonconceptual understanding involves chocolate. Several years ago I watched a documentary about cocoa plantation workers in West Africa. They'd worked for decades picking cocoa beans destined for the chocolate factories of Europe but, amazingly, they'd never tasted chocolate themselves.

They had a good *conceptual* understanding of chocolate. They knew it was delicious and sweet, and came in different flavors, that it was solid to bite into but melted in the mouth.

There was probably little about chocolate they didn't know, at least on an intellectual level.

What made the documentary interesting was that the crew who made it had brought chocolate with them. They gave the workers bars to unwrap, and began to film. You can imagine the broad smiles that lit up the faces of the plantation workers as they tasted chocolate for the very first time. No amount of conceptual knowledge had prepared them for the delightfulness of the nonconceptual experience. The taste of chocolate, vivid and wonderful, far surpassed description. Who cared about conceptual definitions when you could enjoy the delicious experience?

So it is with mind. Words can't do it justice. No matter how accurate or beautifully expressed, no amount of conceptual understanding can approach a nonconceptual experience. Nor should we allow ourselves to get caught up in conceptual notions when their only purpose is to help us arrive at a nonconceptual result. As Vietnamese master Thich Nhat Hanh writes in *The Miracle of Mindfulness*, "The finger which points at the moon isn't the moon itself."[3]

When we abide in the experience of mind we find that many adjectives we use to describe it are about as helpful as calling chocolate "sweet" and "delicious." Well, yes it is, but those words only hint at the full-blown experience of it. Nevertheless, when talking on the subject of mind, we're necessarily operating at a conceptual level. So how might we describe a subjective experience of mind when our thoughts grow fewer and further between, and we can abide in the space between them?

Two particular qualities of the mind are accessible to us, even when we're just starting out: its clarity and its limitless potential.

Experiencing the clear spaciousness of mind

The clarity of mind, the bare absence that allows any thought, perception, or sensation to arise, is perhaps what we notice initially. The more our concentration improves, and the more we cultivate mental and emotional quiescence—or *shamatha*—the more this quality becomes evident.

Many synonyms are used by meditation teachers and writers in trying to convey this non-conceptual aspect conceptually. These include phrases such as "non-obstructive lucidity," "clarity," and "spaciousness." As the Dalai Lama says:

The conventional nature, abiding condition, or defining characteristic of this phenomenon called "mind"—its lack of form and its ability to allow for an appearance of anything to arise as a cognitive object—is not something to be known through logical reasoning. Rather, we can know it only from the impression we build up through the repeated habit of having our mind be focused on mind—in other words, from direct personal experience.[4]

Advanced meditators report that the clarity of mind takes on a luminosity or brightness as their concentration improves— and along with the glow, a sense of bliss. This experience of mind as light is a natural consequence of meditative concentration and arises as a result of settling into the natural, primordial state of mind. It isn't some kind of religious experience or ecstatic emotional high. It's described by meditators from all backgrounds, secular and religious.

Observing the background of mind: the field from which all arises

The other thing we can observe, even early on, is the paradoxical quality of the space between thoughts. So fixated are we on our thoughts, we think of them as what's really happening in our mind and the space between them as just nothing. When we recognize that thoughts arise from mind itself and are of the same nature as mind, we begin to see this is a false distinction.

What may strike us initially as a void of activity is actually nothing of the kind. In meditation, as we become more acquainted with the background, the context of our thoughts, we experience for ourselves how this "nothing" background is actually the field from which everything arises. It is an infinite expanse of possibility. Rather than being focused on individual waves, our gaze broadens to see an ocean of limitless potential. As B. Alan Wallace observes:

> The background is relatively constant from one session to the next, but it is not static or immutable. In fact, sometimes it seems pregnant with potential, a field in bloom, or an effervescence about to explode! This space is not an empty nothingness—it's not flat empty. Such qualifiers point to a paradox: emptiness is full.[5]

The feeling of mind watching mind

One of the reasons this meditation is so powerful and, once you have a taste for it, so compelling, is that we keep making fresh discoveries about our own mind that are not only happiness-creating but also increasingly shift the way we experience reality. The discovery that the gap between thoughts is the opposite of an empty void is one revelatory paradox.

Another is that far from being a purely cognitive exercise, this meditation evokes feelings of profound well-being and tranquillity. Words typically used to describe a state of deep meditative concentration on mind include "great bliss," "abiding peacefulness" and "radiant luminosity." As already noted by meditation masters including Thich Nhat Hanh, these terms are merely conceptual fingers pointing towards a numinous reality far more powerful than any label. Only direct personal experience can give us a true sense of what's meant by these terms. Like the cocoa plantation workers, we must actually taste the experience if we're to begin to understand the full significance of these descriptors and the paradox that a state free of thought can also be one of oceanic good feeling.

At the start of this chapter I quoted Heraclitus, a Greek philosopher who was, in broad terms, a contemporary of Buddha and whose observation is one with which Buddha would have readily agreed: "No man ever steps in the same river twice; for it is not the same river, and he is not the same man." This idea certainly applies to the experience of mind watching mind. The flow of clarity and cognition we observe is never the same as it was last week, yesterday, or even an hour ago. It may have the overall appearance of being the same, but the actual experience is always a fresh one.

What's more, we're not the same observer, if for no other reason than that we've gained slightly more experience in this particular activity than an hour ago, yesterday, or last week. Constantly, subtly evolving, the more our concentration improves and the greater our experience in this meditation, the further we can advance into the inexpressible, radiant benevolence beyond concept.

How can mind meditate on mind?

People sometimes ask how mind can meditate on itself.

Traditionally in the West we have five sensory perceptions—sight, hearing, smell, taste, and touch. In the East there's a sixth—mental perception. This is the perception we use to observe all mental activity such as thoughts, images, remembered lyrics or music, dreams, and so on. This "sixth sense" is logical in the context of what we might broadly call the inward-focused, subjective science of the East.

In the same way that the outward-focused science of the West demands tools to observe and define external phenomena, in the East, mental perception is the instrument of choice for looking within. Unlike the other senses, only this one can be significantly refined and improved. What's more, there are no known limits to its capabilities.

When we use mental perception to observe our own mind, we feel as though we're using one part of mind to observe the rest, but in truth this is not a real-time observation so much as awareness of what happens a millisecond afterwards. There's no division between a "subject" mind and an "object" mind. There's only one mind and a singular cognition—a formless continuum of clarity and awareness.

As we settle into our practice, we experience moments when we fall into a state of non-duality. The experience is no longer so much one of "me watching my mind" as more simply of "being here." There is no I and no mind, no subject and no object. There's only awareness, pure presence.

This state is one of timelessness. When we come back to "me watching my mind" we may find that quite a long time has elapsed, even though there was no subjective feeling of time passing. This non-dual experience is not one of zoned-out vacuity. We feel the profound stillness and radiant well-being already described, only when we pay attention to the flow of moments, deliberately and nonjudgmentally, there's no "self" or "me" experiencing it. We can avoid inserting an unnecessary "I" into what's happening. We abide, simply, in the boundless here and now.

···· Where do "I" go when I meditate on mind? ····

What happens to the entity that goes by many names—"me," "myself," "my persona," "my psyche"—when we meditate? The term "acquired personality" is a useful definition here. All our biographical details, cultural and family conditioning, genetic and epigenetic influences, individual narratives, likes, dislikes, hopes, fears, and quirks might be assembled under the label "acquired personality." It's what makes "me" unique— just like everyone else!

In his book *Minding Closely*, B. Alan Wallace likens the acquired personality to a snowflake, a metaphor that lends itself to the following analogy:

> *if we melt any snowflake, its fundamental ingredient is simply water. Similarly, when you or anyone "melts" the psyche by using shamatha, and it settles back into the substrate consciousness from which it arose, then the three traits that you or anyone will find, regardless of genetic and cultural background, are that the substrate consciousness is blissful, luminous, and nonconceptual.*[6]

This process, here so vividly described, is wonderfully liberating! When we can enjoy some level of mental quiescence and abide in the tranquil clarity of mind, however briefly, we directly experience for ourselves the more subtle state of consciousness: the essential nature of our own mind.

The Buddhist view is that this is the formless continuum from which all else arises. A taste of this subtle, primordial mind is all we need to recognize that our acquired personality, which we generally suppose our self to be, is nothing but an elaborate confection.

There is, of course, a physical basis to this confection—although as we get older we come to realize that any permanence we attach to our bodies is misplaced because they're subject to constant change, rarely for the better. As we head through middle age, the degradation of the physical component of the confection often becomes clearly apparent in the form of burgeoning waistline, sagging body parts, poorer muscle tone, and less lustrous skin!

For most of us, our identity, our notion of who "I" am, is also largely a collection of ideas we have about ourselves, stories and conceptions that build over time, serving to entrench our mistaken belief in a fixed and stable entity called "me." I'm *this* kind of person. I'm conditioned by *these* formative or other experiences. I support *these* values, causes, and organizations. I'm defined by *these* beliefs. The more we build entire anthologies of stories about ourselves and collaborate in creating the anthologies of those around us, the more we create identities that are so concretized we believe they exist independently, with their own qualities and characteristics.

Then we meditate. We discover that every thought we have arises, abides, and passes. There's nothing permanent in our consciousness. Just because we think of something as being like this or like that doesn't mean we'll always do so. Every story we have about ourselves is just that: a story, a current draft.

The most enthusiastic carnivores become vegetarian when they have different ideas about their place in the world around them. Anti-establishment dope-smokers reform to become hardheaded corporate warriors. Social, religious, and political leaders behave in ways that contradict apparently "deeply held beliefs"—*there's* a phrase imbued with apparent permanence! None of this is to deny the impacts of nature, nurture, and conditioning, or the way many of us cast ourselves in particular roles and become more defined by these roles year by year. It's the simple observation that patterns of behavior, mental or otherwise, have no inherent permanence. And neither does the acquired personality. The "I" about whom other people inquire politely is an abstraction, a hypothesis—their version, almost certainly quite different from our own, which itself is open to revision on the basis of something as potentially trivial as a single phone call.

Even though we're so thoroughly invested in our own particular idea of "I" that all it takes is the slightest criticism to make us feel angry or upset, even though we'll make the most incredible sacrifices to prove the worth of "I," even though some people are so despairing of their "I" that they choose to end their own life, when we meditate on mind we expose this entity's awful secret: "I" is just an idea, just another concept that arises, abides, and passes. Ask me about "I" and I'll tell you. Catch me in a different moment and my story of "I" will be different.

So where does this "I" go when I meditate? Nowhere, really, because it wasn't there to begin with—unless you happened to be thinking about yourself, in which case, as you settle your mind, those thoughts too will pass.

This understanding of self was first proposed by Buddha, whose extraordinary insight is summed up by Buddhist teacher and author Stephen Batchelor as follows:

> Gotama [Buddha] did for the self what Copernicus did for the earth: he put it in its rightful place, despite its continuing to appear just as it did before. Gotama no more rejected the existence of the self than Copernicus rejected the existence of the earth. Instead, rather than regarding it as a fixed, non-contingent point around which everything else turned, he recognized that each self was a fluid, contingent process just like everything else.[7]

Coming home to our primordial mind

When we relax and let go, there is no "I." We become free of thoughts about our acquired personality. Slowly, and over time, at first in only brief glimpses, the veil of ideas and concepts obscuring our mind disappears—"like morning mist," in the words of one classic text. Revealed is the nature of our primordial mind, its sheer luminosity now brightly manifest. The more vivid our attention, the more radiantly is mind evident.

Unlike the stories we have about ourselves, this state isn't an idea subject to revision at any time. It's beyond concept. For that very reason it defies verbal description and must be experienced directly.

Gradually, we come to understand the reality that our mind does not, in fact, occupy our head, but is truly boundless and all-encompassing. The infinite field of all possibilities is as much a flow of feelings as of cognition, and the tone of those feelings engenders profound tranquility, well-being, even bliss. We have the sense that the nature of our boundless, potential-filled luminosity is one of pure, great love. Our innate wish is to stay connected to this awareness and in harmony with it.

To encounter that state is revelatory. Even though our stay is only temporary, it has the potential to be life-changing because something shifts. What we've experienced, in a way of such vivid clarity that there can be no denying our experience, we know to be true and enduring. We sense it is omnipresent, although usually obscured beneath layers of cognition. We have first-hand, if limited, knowledge of a subtle dimension of being we have previously been too busy to notice. The veil has lifted and we have discovered our own true nature.

From understanding
arises compassion

Even though we may embark on our meditative journey motivated by *self*-discovery, what arises when we encounter our own true nature is yet another paradox: compassion for others. The nature of our mind is one of softness, gentleness. No matter how forbidding an exterior we may choose to present to the world or the nature of our acquired personality, when all this conceptual elaboration is stripped away, the nature of the mind is the same for us all. And once we've experienced this for ourselves, it's natural for us to seek to avoid behavior that's dissonant with it and to cultivate actions that support this inner wellspring of contentment.

In Chapter 4 we looked at research studies showing that meditators are better at empathizing with others, more effective at paying attention to others and reading their moods. The development of empathy arises from several factors—yes, an enhanced ability to focus on the other person because there's less agitation in our own mind—but over time also a genuine concern for others supported by the recognition that the same thing that causes us suffering is a cause of suffering for them, too. The critical difference is that we now have some experience that things aren't what they seem.

Our problems are caused when we buy into our acquired personality, treating it as though it's permanent, independent—"the real me." Our growing experience that this unstable anthology of stories and qualities is nothing more than that helps us let go of our attachment to it. Little by little we become less hung up if others criticize "me," less angry when they seek to advance their own interests at "my" expense, less frustrated or depressed when "I" don't get what "I" want—because we've started to see through the illusion of "I" and, instead, to experience the panoramic radiance that lies beneath such passing conceptions.

We can also see the great suffering endured by others because they haven't experienced this radiance. Given that they believe their acquired personality to be their true nature, it's hardly surprising they get themselves into trouble, because the whole basis of the way that their "I" relates to the world is flawed. They're victims, first and foremost, of their own ideas about themselves, ideas that may accord with conventional assumptions, but that just aren't sustainable if they were to experience their own minds directly.

If love is the wish to give happiness to others and compassion the wish to free others from their suffering, it becomes quite natural to wish to become more loving and compassionate, because we recognize that just as we are, others are, too. For all of us seeking happiness and the avoidance of dissatisfaction, our greatest challenges lie not, as we believe, in the world around us, but in our own mistaken assumptions about ourselves.

As we progress towards the river mouth of our mindfulness journey, we become aware that our ultimate destination is beyond abiding in the pristine luminosity of mind alone. As our experience of non-duality deepens, we recognize that only when everyone else is released from the constraints of their unknowing limitations will we be able to abide in the oceanic bliss of transcendence.

Meditation checklist

1 *Establish your physical posture.* Your back is straight, your legs are crossed on a cushion or planted on the floor, hands resting like a pair of shells, shoulders rolled back, arms loose by your sides, head tilted according to your state of mind, tip of tongue on the roof of the mouth, face relaxed, and eyes shut.

2 *Establish your psychological posture.* Give yourself permission not to think about your usual concerns. The next ten-minute period is time out.

3 *Mentally establish your motivation.* Repeat two or three times either:

By the practice of this meditation
I am becoming calm and relaxed,
Happier and more efficient in all that I do,
Both for my own sake as well as for others.

or:

To the Buddha, Dharma, and Sangha,
I go for refuge until becoming enlightened.
By the practice of giving and so on,
May I attain enlightenment to benefit all beings.

4 *Settle your mind using breath-based meditation.* Focus on your breath using either the breath-counting or nine-cycle breathing meditation. Use mindfulness and awareness as usual, and bring your attention back to your breath every time it wanders.

5 *Once your mind has settled to some extent, change the object of meditation to mind itself.* Simply sit and be aware of what's happening in your mind. When thoughts arise, acknowledge, accept, and let go. Observe how thoughts can't survive if you don't give them your attention.

6 *If useful, ask yourself "Where did that thought come from?"*

7 *Wordlessly and without concept, abide in the nature of your own mind.* Be aware how thoughts naturally arise and dissolve

back into mind, how they're of the same nature as mind. No-tice what qualities mind has.

8 *End the session.* However good or bad your concentration during the session, try especially hard to focus strongly at the end—finish like a winner. Afterwards, repeat your affirmation two or three times:

By the practice of this meditation
I am becoming calm and relaxed,
Happier and more efficient in all that I do,
Both for my own sake as well as for others.

or:

To the Buddha, Dharma, and Sangha,
I go for refuge until becoming enlightened.
By the practice of giving and so on,
May I attain enlightenment to benefit all beings.

Allow yourself a few moments to open your eyes and come back to the room.

Further inspiration

When I practice this meditation, I sometimes find it useful to draw on the wisdom of meditation masters who've gone before us. Below is some of the advice I personally find invaluable, which I hope you'll find similarly inspiring.

You may like to choose just one of the following verses per meditation session, and if your mind becomes agitated, open your eyes, read the verse, then return to mind watching mind with additional inspiration.

- From *Tilopa's Mahamudra Instruction to Naropa in Twenty-eight Verses* (tenth century), translated by and reproduced with kind permission of Keith Dowman:

Gazing intently into the empty sky, vision ceases;
Likewise, when mind gazes into mind itself,
The train of discursive and conceptual thought ends
And supreme enlightenment is gained.

Like the morning mist that dissolves into thin air,
Going nowhere but ceasing to be,
Waves of conceptualization, all the mind's creation, dissolve,
When you behold your mind's true nature.

Pure space has neither color nor shape
And it cannot be stained either black or white;
So also, mind's essence is beyond both color and shape
And it cannot be sullied by black or white deeds.

Although space has been designated "empty,"
In reality it is inexpressible;
Although the nature of mind is called "clear light,"
Its every ascription is baseless verbal fiction.

The mind's original nature is like space;
It pervades and embraces all things under the sun.
Be still and stay relaxed in genuine ease,
Be quiet and let sound reverberate as an echo,
Keep your mind silent and watch the ending of all worlds.[8]

• From Maitripa (eleventh-century yogi and teacher):

If you wish to realize the meaning that is beyond intellect, with nothing to be done, root out your limited awareness and settle starkly into pure awareness. Plunge into the waters of this pristine lucidity, unsullied by any stain of conceptual thinking. Settle in mind's own state in the space that is neither the appearance-making and appearance that have ceased nor the ones about to be established.[9]

• Similes to help develop *shamatha* from the First Panchen Lama (Khedrup Je; fourteenth century):

Like an eagle in the sky. *Unlike a small bird that needs to constantly flap its wings, a great eagle soars with the currents as it glides aloft. In the same way, soar in the clear light of mind with relaxed ease. While maintaining clarity and sharpness there is no need to exercise mindfulness and awareness in a frenetic way.*

Like a great ship on the ocean. *Even though the wind may blow and waves may bump up against the vessel, they are powerless to send the ship off course. Likewise, even when thoughts arise in your mind, don't become involved in them. They are powerless to develop into full-blown conceptual thoughts that disturb your equanimity.*[10]

12

Healing and the mind

....

It's supposed to be a professional secret, but I will tell
you anyway. We doctors do nothing. We only help
and encourage the doctor within.

DR. ALBERT SCHWEITZER[1]

....

I t's no coincidence that the two words "medication" and
"meditation" are only one letter different: both come from
the same Latin root, *medeor*, meaning "to heal." While
on the subject of etymology, "heal" is a Germanic word that
comes to us through Old English, and its literal meaning is "to
make whole." Whether we're medicating or meditating, therefore, our purpose is the same—to achieve wholeness.

In Chapter 4 we looked at the powerful benefits of meditation according to a wide range of physiological metrics. Our
understanding of the possibilities for healing expand all the
more when we understand how different interpretations of
reality impact on our bodies. This is even more the case when
we cease to think of mind as synonymous with our brain and

experience it as having the qualities of an energetic field or flow from which everything arises.

As we saw in Chapter 4, extensive research has already established the impact of mind on our physiological functioning, whether measured in terms of blood pressure, hormone production, or telomerase activity. Is it really such a great leap to suggest that our state of mind, whether happy or unhappy, is vital in determining our state of ease or disease, or that mindfulness can also play a critical role in healing? If so, how might we set about making a tool of mindfulness, consciously taking charge of our mind to optimize our chances of healing or wholeness?

The outsourcing of healing

In the West, with our culturally ingrained dualistic notions of body and mind, we've traditionally thought of our physical health as being an area that, because of our poor knowledge, is best left to the experts. When something goes wrong we need to consult a doctor, or perhaps a specialist, who has far better understanding of our physiology than we do. This view has given rise to an interesting phenomenon, which we'll explore later in this chapter. But an unfortunate consequence for some people is that they see themselves as the victim of health problems over which only medical professionals have control.

Not so long ago an elderly lady I knew quite well, who was finding it painful to walk any distance at all, complained bitterly to me about the shortcomings of her doctors. She'd repeatedly asked them to fix a variety of health problems, but despite a mindboggling array of pills, she was only getting worse. What was wrong with these people?

As it happened, the lady had had a quadruple bypass some years before, after which her doctors had advised her to give up smoking and take regular exercise. She still smoked and led an almost entirely sedentary life. She had no interest in changing her lifestyle. Perhaps at some level she accepted that her behavior had consequences, but at her advanced age she intended to live as she damned well pleased. The impression I always had of her, however, was one of genuine disappointment at the inadequacies of her doctors.

Dr. Lissa Rankin, a medical doctor and author of *Mind Over Medicine*, talks about exactly this paradigm and says it's one in which most people are willing to function. She writes:

> The alternative—that you have more power to heal your own body than you've ever imagined—lobs the responsibility for health back into your court, and many people feel like that's just too much responsibility. It's much easier to hand over your power and hope someone smarter, wiser, and more experienced can "fix" you.[2]

The shift to participatory medicine

It's true that while many of us are happy to pay lip-service to the idea of taking responsibility for our own health, we're often less consistent when it comes to putting theory into practice. The financial modeling of gyms is premised on the fact that of the many hundreds who sign twelve-month contracts, few will remain as regulars after that first flush of enthusiasm.

Even those who take diet and exercise quite seriously can experience emotional turmoil in the face of illness. There's something strongly disempowering about the diagnosis of a disease, especially when you thought you were taking good care of yourself. No one knowingly invites illness upon themselves. What's more, as soon as we engage with the medical world, we're in foreign territory where we must quickly master a new language, abide by unfamiliar practices, and rely for guidance on our doctor.

Given that we didn't consciously seek out disease, the notion that we might consciously be able to promote recovery may seem unlikely. But the research of recent decades supports this very notion. Where we keep tripping ourselves up, it would seem, is on mind–body duality.

Health advice usually focuses almost entirely on the physical, in particular the importance of a balanced diet, regular exercise, and the avoidance of toxins including cigarettes, drugs, and excessive alcohol. Little detailed attention has traditionally been paid to the state of a person's mind. Interestingly, when it is, the solution provided tends to be a physical one, such as a prescription for Prozac, Valium, and so on, designed to change our biochemistry.

But what if mind, as Buddha himself suggested, really is the forerunner of all events? What if, even though we didn't consciously seek out disease, it only came into being because of our mind? And what if mind has the power to affect our physiological functioning, even those mechanisms below the threshold of consciousness, to promote healing or wholeness?

This is the premise of a new field in which individuals, instead of fully outsourcing their health to the experts, reclaim some of the responsibility themselves, and instead of viewing disease as treatable through only physical means, also bring to bear the energetic power of their own consciousness. This emerging field is called by some "participatory medicine."

What causes disease?

In the West, our instinct is to seek out physical causes for disease. We train our doctors to become expert in identifying those bacteria and viruses that cause infection, the modifiable lifestyle factors that lead to thickened arteries or the non-modifiable risk factors, usually genetic, that predispose us to certain conditions.

While I don't wish to detract from the efficiency of conventional medicine, which is most people's first port of call in a health crisis—and definitely mine—the truth is that there are fewer answers when we dig deeper behind these identifiable causes.

Why is it that a number of people can be exposed to the same bacteria, but only some of them will succumb? Okay, their immune system is compromised, but why? How can a person be exposed to the same virus on eight occasions without mishap, but on the ninth become infected? Why does one person get a cancer associated with a high genetic risk factor while their twin is unaffected? How can two equally unhealthy individuals have bad diets, but one has a massive heart attack while the other happily continues their daily visits to the fast food outlet?

Genes and epigenetics

Most diagnostic sessions with a doctor include a family history—a hunt for the genetic origins of illness. Genes were once believed to be all important in determining all manner of outcomes, including predisposition to disease. You were your genes. Then came the Human Genome Project, which instead of decoding the activity of the 120,000-plus genes that were thought to make up the human genome, identified a dramatically lower gene count of at most 25,000. In the words of cell biologist Bruce Lipton, "There are simply not enough genes to account for the complexity of human life or of human disease."[3]

Subsequent findings in the field of epigenetics, which examines how proteins produced by some genes can alter the expression (switching on or off) of others, have revealed that the causality of genetic coding is far less straightforward than previously believed. Osteoporosis, once thought to be caused by a single mutant gene, was shown to involve the interaction of no fewer than 500 genes. Importantly, genes themselves can be switched on or off. Studies of identical twins carried out by Professor Tim Spector at King's College, London yielded findings with powerful implications for genetic determinists. According to Professor Spector, "the heritability of your age at death is only about 25%. Similarly, there is only a 30% chance that if one identical twin gets heart disease the other one will as well, while the figure for rheumatoid arthritis is only about 15%."[4]

Looking to our genes may help tell part of the story, but not the whole story.

Lifestyle factors

The village of Roseto in Pennsylvania has become associated in recent years with a study by general practitoner Stewart

Wolf and sociologist John Bruhn, whose work is examined by Malcolm Gladwell in his book *Outliers*.[5] In this small village, the death rate from heart disease in men over sixty-five was about half the average in the United States as a whole. In addition, in Roseto there was no suicide, alcoholism, drug addiction, or peptic ulcers. In many ways, Roseto was strongly atypical of mainstream America.

Wolf set about trying to find out why this was so. Along the way, he discovered that the diet of Roseto citizens, many of whom were originally from Roseto Valfortore in Italy, was less than optimal. They ate pizza using thick bread dough, enjoyed sweets all year round, and a very high 41 percent of their calories were derived from fat. Many smoked heavily and many were obese.

Their genes provided no explanation—Rosetans who lived in other parts of the United States didn't share their same good health. Nor was it the location: in the nearby towns of Bangor and Nazareth, death rates from heart disease were three times greater.

Instead it emerged that "the Rosetans were healthy because . . . of the world they had created for themselves in their tiny little town in the hills."[6] Many homes were shared by three generations. Mass at Our Lady of Mount Carmel involved everyone. There was a strong sense of community, an egalitarian ethos that meant that whatever their individual circumstances, everyone felt they belonged.

Lifestyle factors that would automatically have placed them at very high risk in other circumstances seemed to have been mitigated by a less tangible but more powerful sense of well-being. The lesson we can draw from this is that along with the traditional external predictors of illness, other inner factors must be taken into account.

Stress

If forced to nominate just one single inner factor that contributes to illness, we would more than likely choose stress. As body–mind medicine expert Dr. Craig Hassed of Monash University in Melbourne, Australia, notes, the long-term over-activation of the stress response creates a physiological wear and tear on the body, resulting in immune dysregulation, including lowered defenses against infection and increased inflammation; the hardening of arteries leading to cardiovascular disease; high blood pressure, hypertension, and increased weight around the trunk; osteoporosis; loss of brain cells and accelerated aging, predisposing one to Alzheimer's later in life; and chronic depression and anxiety.[7]

There's a widespread belief in the community that stress can cause certain cancers. While this belief is understandable, epidemiological studies into what causes cancer have yet to prove this to be true. Some studies suggest a stress link, but other studies of groups of people who have gone through very stressful experiences, such as losing a child or being imprisoned in a concentration camp, have shown them to be at no greater risk of cancer than the general population.

Part of the difficulty of validating the link is that, as seen in previous chapters, stress is caused not so much by external events as by our interpretation of them. How one person comes to terms with even something as significant as the loss of a child will be very different from how another does. The true measure of stress is therefore not the event itself so much as the interpretations of that event. These are much more difficult to measure.

The havoc played with our immune system by stress, along with its inflammatory impact, certainly support a physiological explanation of how cancer may be triggered, and many cancer patients attribute their illness to one severely stressful experience triggering a dramatic drop in their sense of well-being. Some researchers contend that even if stress isn't a direct cause of cancer, it may be an indirect cause: if people respond to stress by smoking, drinking too much, and neglecting their diet, these factors increase their cancer risk.

Stress, and the wide-ranging damage it does to our physical well-being, is number one on the list of psychological causes of disease. But there are others.

As we've already seen in the case of the Rosetans, a strong sense of belonging and being engaged with the local community can do wonders for our health and longevity. It can also compensate for other risk factors such as obesity and a poor diet. But developed society is heading in the opposite direction, with increasing numbers of single-person households, including a great demographic wave of aging baby boomers, many of whom are destined to live on their own.

Living alone and being lonely are, of course, two entirely different things. The level to which we feel socially engaged and need to feel socially engaged differs widely from person to person. Like stress, loneliness is ultimately defined by each of us personally. What we do know from the work of psychologist John Cacioppo and others is that people who feel lonely are physiologically different from those who don't. Specifically, they have a higher diastolic blood pressure (the lower number in a blood pressure reading) in response to stress, an impaired immune system, and a greater inflammatory response, along with producing more of the stress hormone cortisol. They have higher rates of heart disease, breast cancer, and Alzheimer's disease, and have even been shown to have higher mortality rates after coronary artery bypass surgery.[8]

Most of us who have elderly parents or relatives living alone know from personal experience how stressed they may get in response to what we regard as trivial incidents, how anxious they may become about, for example, the prospect of a long journey—something to which we attach little if any anxiety. Their world shrinks so much that molehills are magnified into mountains. Without a familiar hand to hold or someone to provide a contrary point of view, they continuously play negative narrative loops in their minds, and these just become more and more entrenched.

According to Robert Putnam in his book *Bowling Alone*, "As a rough rule of thumb, if you belong to no groups but decide to join one, you cut your risk of dying over the next year in half. If you smoke and belong to no groups, it's a toss-up statistically whether you should stop smoking or start joining."[9] Suffice it to say, most people find it a lot easier to start joining!

When we feel a sense of acceptance, belonging, and love, we're in a context in which we can thrive. The opposite, loneliness, is as bad for our health as smoking.

Pessimism

"An optimist sees the doughnut, a pessimist the hole," goes the old adage. Martin Seligman, famous for his work on positive psychology and optimism, provides a more detailed definition of the difference between optimistic and pessimistic thinking. Specifically, it boils down to how permanently, pervasively, and personally both good and bad news are perceived.

An optimist, faced with a negative event, will believe its effects to be temporary, of only limited impact, and to reflect little, if at all, on themselves. Faced with the same bad news, the pessimist sees the negative event as permanently blighting their lives, ruining everything, and being personal—"This always happens to me" or "It's all my fault."

When something positive happens, the pessimist regards it as temporary, specific, and having nothing to do with them—a brief interlude of sunlight before heavy cloud cover resumes. By contrast, an optimist sees permanence and pervasiveness in the happy occurrence, not to mention the fact that it reflects their own wonderfulness and good fortune.

Where this gets really interesting is the impact of optimism and pessimism on health. A fascinating analysis of longitudinal data by Martin Seligman and Chris Peterson showed that by the age of forty-five, pessimists were already less healthy than optimists, getting sick younger and more severely. By age sixty, the pessimists were significantly sicker.

Dr. Lissa Rankin summarizes other health differences:

pessimists are more susceptible to depression, more likely to experience barriers to professional success, less likely to experience pleasure, more likely to endure challenges in their relationships, and more likely to get sick. Studies show that optimists catch fewer infectious diseases than pessimists, have stronger immune systems and lower blood pressures, live longer, and are less likely to suffer from cardiac disease.[10]

One study by Harvard psychologist Laura Kubzansky followed 1,300 men over a ten-year period and found that heart disease among the pessimists was double that among the optimists. Once again, this difference is about the same as that recorded between smokers and non-smokers.[11]

Mindfulness is wellness

The quantifiable findings of many studies over recent decades show that disease may be caused as much by mental factors as by physical ones. Stress, loneliness, and pessimism are a few of the factors we have looked at, but there are others, toxic relationships and financial worries among them.

If the best way to deal with a particular disease is not to get it in the first place, then along with minimizing external risks such as poor diet and a sedentary lifestyle, we also need to minimize the risks to our mental well-being. Part of this is about nurturing healthy, positive relationships with strong networks of friends, family, colleagues, and even pets. The Roseto study demonstrates the enormous power of feeling a sense of connectedness and belonging.

Minimizing external stressors in our daily lives where necessary and possible may also help our mental well-being. We can maintain a state of dysfunctional busy-ness for only so long before something has to give. Sometimes, in spite of how we feel, we don't need to change our whole life to reduce the stress. Changes as subtle as taking two nights off a week from TV and social media, outsourcing domestic chores where possible, or learning to say no to work and social invitations are enough to help take the lid off the pressure cooker.

Of course, the ultimate stress-buster is to live more mindfully. When we can find ten minutes each morning to practice abiding in a state of calm clarity, when we mindfully enjoy every cup of coffee we drink and each meal we eat, when our days are punctuated by moments of paying attention to the present deliberately and nonjudgmentally, we feel far less under siege.

What's more, as we become more aware of what's going on in our mind, we become more adept at managing our own thoughts. Negative or stress-inducing interpretations of what's going on may still habitually arise, but now we also have the ability to counter them, to recognize irrational negativity and move towards a position of greater equanimity.

Best of all, if we can deepen our experience of the true nature of mind itself, we find it easier to let go of the real source of our unhappiness: our own self-obsession. Stress, loneliness, pessimism, financial worries, and unhappy relationships all have one thing in common: they're all about "me." "*I've* got far too much to do before we hit the deadline," "No one ever invites *me* out," "Nothing in *my* life ever works out the way I want it to," "*I'm* sinking in debt and I'm letting my family down," "Why isn't she as nice to *me* as she is to the cat?"

When we understand the true nature of mind, we start to see these thoughts merely as thoughts instead of engaging with them. They arise, abide, and pass. They have no substance and certainly no power unless we give it to them. Increasingly, we also realize that the "me" to which they all refer is actually a hypothesis. Of course there's a conventional "me" on whom colleagues or clients may be relying. That version of "me" is almost certainly quite different from our own, a version over which we have only modest influence and that's probably of limited interest to them. It's *our* version of "me" that causes us the most stress and heartache.

Which is why it comes as a relief to discover that this version is as transient as a cloud in the sky. Focus on the cloud and the result is uncertain. Focus on the sky and we discover clarity, boundlessness and a profound sense of well-being. In the words of the fourteenth-century Tibetan Buddhist sage Shantideva:

If all the injury,
Fear and pain in this world
Arise from grasping at a self,
Then what use is that great ghost to me?

Living a meaningful life

The recognition described by Shantideva leads directly to the Tibetan Buddhist prescription for a meaningful life, one that optimizes mental well-being: instead of thinking so much about ourselves, we should deliberately think more about others. The Buddhist definition of love is *the wish to give happiness to others*, while compassion is *the wish to free others from suffering*. When the Dalai Lama says "my religion is loving kindness," he isn't being fluffy, he's referring to the deliberate cultivation of others-focused practices of body, speech, and mind.

As our thoughts turn to others, we don't usually have to look too far to see how tough many people are doing it compared to us. Our own problems seem smaller and more manageable. When we practice compassion, we behave in a way that's more congruent with the true nature of our mind once the "me"-centric clouds have blown over the horizon.

Looking for empirical evidence, recent studies show that we feel happier when we include others in our thoughts. Donating even small amounts of money, time, or blood quite measurably enhance our own feelings of happiness. Being kind, generous, and attentive to the needs of others isn't just some religious ideal propagated to inspire altruism or keep a grip on society. The wonderful paradox is that we, ourselves, are the first to benefit.

These themes are explored in much more detail in my book *Enlightenment to Go: Shantideva and the Power of Compassion to Transform Your Life*.[12] For the purposes of this chapter, it's enough to summarize that mental well-being is as much about the amount of airplay we give to others as we give to ourselves. The more we can broaden our perspective and engage with the bigger picture, the more pervasive our sense of well-being is likely to be.

In his book *The World As I See It*, Albert Einstein wrote: "The true value of a human being is determined primarily by the measure and the sense in which he has attained to liberation from the self."[13] One of the greatest thinkers of the twentieth century concurred with his eastern counterpart of 2,500 years earlier, Buddha: most of us find vastly greater meaning and purpose in our lives when we can look beyond our own narrow self-interest and encompass the interests of others in whatever we do.

Healing the body with the mind

Mental factors play an important role in helping prevent disease, but what if we're already ill? Once physical dysfunction sets in, is it too late for something as ethereal as mental activity to help?

The answer to this is an unequivocal no. There's no shortage of illustrations highlighting the healing power of the mind, of which the placebo effect is perhaps the most obvious example. From the Latin "I shall please"—referring to the patient's attitude to the doctor—in clinical drug trials the placebo effect is an accepted principle that typically one-third of control patients who are given inert pills with no active ingredients will respond as if they'd received the benefits of the new drug being tested on a sample group. Symptoms disappear, pain evaporates, and healing is achieved because the patients believe they are receiving an effective treatment.

The placebo effect works across an astonishing variety of health problems: asthma, colitis, infertility, allergies, endocrine disorders, mental health conditions such as anxiety and depression, Parkinson's, insomnia, cardiac symptoms such as angina, and, most effectively, pain disorders. In one case a placebo was shown to be more effective than certain prescription antidepressant medications. Controversially, the clinical benefits of antidepressants as a general category are considered by many in the medical profession to be not much different from those of placebos.[14]

The placebo effect goes much further than pills alone. Dr. Bruce Moseley, an orthopedic surgeon who specializes in helping people with debilitating knee pain, carried out an astonishing study of sham surgery in which patients were sedated, underwent incisions made to replicate real surgery, and shown a tape recording of someone else's surgery on a video monitor. After a while, Dr. Moseley stitched their knees back up again.

When comparing the response rates among patients who'd had sham versus actual surgery, Dr. Moseley found that in both cases, resolution of knee pain was about one-third. The results of his clinical trial, published in the *New England Journal of Medicine*, showed that just as many people recovered simply because they believed they'd received surgery.[15]

To date, there's no data on the use of placebos to treat cancer and other potentially life-threatening diseases. When new drugs are trialed, they're usually tested against existing treatments. Giving cancer patients a sugar-pill placebo would almost certainly be regarded as unethical.

A number of explanations are offered about why placebos work. The most likely is that our belief that we will be healed itself creates the causes for our healing. It could be that our faith in an authority figure in a white coat prescribing a particular course of treatment may work its magic. So, too, could the emotional support we receive from doctors, nurses, or others. Or, quite possibly, all of these factors combined.

One Harvard Medical School study showed that the response of people with irritable bowel syndrome to a placebo increased from 44 percent to 62 percent in cases where doctors treated their patients with "warmth, attention, and confidence."[16] Sixty-two percent is an astonishingly high figure. It would certainly be enough to get any drug onto pharmaceutical rosters.

This finding, published relatively recently, confirms the quote of Dr. Albert Schweitzer at the head of this chapter about the role of doctors. Could it really be that their primary role is to give us a reason to believe we will be cured, with the actual treatment they prescribe being secondary? This would certainly help explain non-medical treatments such as reiki and homeopathy, which are as routinely lambasted by clinicians as they are vigorously advocated by their beneficiaries. Perhaps it's not the treatments themselves so much as a patient's belief in the process, or the practitioner, that heals.

An interesting thing about placebos is that they're not the preserve of the unintelligent or gullible. Anyone is likely to benefit from the placebo effect, irrespective of their IQ or background. It's also the case that placebos work without the patient having any knowledge at all of the precise physiological changes required to resolve an illness. It's not as though healing only occurs among those patients with a detailed understanding of what changes need to occur. Placebos work because of patients" belief. All else can be left to the body–mind field.

The curious revelations of multiple personalities

While the placebo is among the most common examples of the impact of the mind on health problems, it's not the only one. Another is well established in the world of dissociative identity disorders (also known as multiple identity disorders), where a patient in one state may suffer from a particular condition, such as diabetes, but as soon as their non-diabetic alter ego takes over, their entire physiology changes and blood sugar levels return to normal.

The same body but an altered state of mind yields two completely different physiological results. Psychiatrist Bennett Braun described how one of his patients, Timmy, was able to drink orange juice with no ill effect, while his other personalities were extremely allergic to it, and if they took over after he'd had only a single sip, he'd break out in blistering hives.[17]

Another patient suffered a bee sting to which one of their personalities had an extreme allergic reaction. The fortuitous flipping of personality to another state quickly resolved the problem before the patient had to be admitted to hospital.

The advice of cancer survivors

What we can learn from all this is that mind not only can heal, but also routinely does so. It would be invaluable to know more precisely what mental elements are required to make this happen. A number of interrelated reasons are usually given why these elements have not yet been found. These include a lack of funding, the vested interests of Big Pharma, and the dogmatic materialism of the medical community. Hopefully, as attitudes shift, so will the level of research into this most promising field.

So what do we do in the meantime?

Ian Gawler is one of Australia's most famous cancer survivors. His Gawler Foundation has helped many thousands of people through support programs for the past three decades. A few years ago he conducted a survey of thirty-five long-term cancer survivors. All of them had been seriously ill and had been given short-term prognoses—but despite all odds had turned their difficulties around and were alive and well ten years later.

In the survey they were asked to rank those factors they believed to have been most important to their recovery. The kinds of factors included such things as medical treatment, natural therapies, overcoming the fear of dying, forgiveness, nutrition, meditation, and others.

Apparently the question didn't get quite the response the researchers had predicted—most people rated many variables highly. As Gawler observes, "Turning around a major illness is not a casual affair. It does take work. These people were committed. They did a lot, and they rated highly the value of many things that they did do."[18]

Nevertheless, three factors did stand out way above the others. They were diet, meditation, and the development of a spiritual life. The former patients were also asked what advice they would give to people newly diagnosed. Unsurprisingly, the results were very similar: diet, meditation, the aim to find meaning and purpose in life, and also a well-run self-help group.

The experience of this battle-hardened group of survivors supports the thesis that the same factors that support well-being and the prevention of disease when we're healthy also promote healing when we're sick. If we wish to play an active role in our recovery, then alongside the advice of our medical team, there are other things we can do to return to wholeness.

Diet and support groups, while evidently important, are outside the scope of this book. Readers will find these subjects covered in many resources, not least of which is Ian Gawler's own book, *You Can Conquer Cancer*, which I recommend to anyone facing this disease.

How meditation and mindfulness support healing

What about the role of meditation—and its resultant mindfulness—specifically? Readers who've come this far will already have a fair idea of why meditation has such a vital role to play in healing, but let's summarize the key reasons.

Meditation triggers the relaxation response, enabling the body to repair itself

"The relaxation response," as Dr. Herbert Benson of Harvard Medical School first termed it, is a state that helps maximize our body's capacity for self-repair. It short-circuits the stress cycle, enabling changes in body chemistry, in particular switching hormone production from stress response to a focus on boosting our immune systems. Meditation is anti-inflammatory, it helps prevent cardiovascular illness, and it supports health, longevity, and vitality of both body and mind across a wide range of biological markers.

Meditation reduces the stress of having disease

The diagnosis of a serious illness, such as a degenerative illness, can itself be highly stressful. Patients unable to manage this stress are at greater risk of developing stress-induced physical problems such as high blood pressure, viral infections, headaches, sleeping problems, digestive problems, and anxiety. Efforts to manage this stress by increased drinking or other harmful measures only compromises well-being further.

By contrast, meditation helps us deal with stress by providing not only some level of relief for the periods during which we meditate, but also "off-cushion" relief during the times between sessions. As described in previous chapters, it also opens the door to new ways of defining our consciousness and ourselves, enabling us to interpret what's happening to us in a less existentially threatened way.

Genes can play an important role in determining our likelihood of experiencing disease—but whether these genes are switched on or off is the question. Proto-oncogenes, for example, are linked to cancer, and there are also pro-inflammatory genes. Both of these gene types have negative impacts when their expression becomes dysregulated.

But as Jon Kabat-Zinn explains in his chapter of *The Healing Power of Meditation*, "The evidence is growing that when you take care of yourself in a certain way, including by enacting compassionate presence, you are selecting—not consciously of course—which genes are functioning and which genes are being quiet."[19]

The impact of meditation on epigenetics is still a very new field, but initial evidence suggests that when we meditate, positive changes to gene expression occur beneath the threshold of our awareness. These changes may very well influence the course of our recovery.

Part of the reason so many people struggle to find a sense of meaning in these secular times arises from a lack of clarity about who and what they are. Meditation offers a way to perceive our own true nature directly. When we experience consciousness beyond the cloud cover of our thoughts, we view ourselves in a very different way. Far from being the "me, myself, and I" that's the focus of our ongoing narrative, we experience a dimension beyond the acquired personality that's clear, untainted, and radiant. It's the boundless potential from which every thought and action arises.

What we do with this experience is up to each one of us. Those who are religious may find it deepens their faith. Those who are not may become aware that there's more to being human than matter alone: an energetic counterpart must also be accounted for. However we respond, meditation provides access to a dimension of experience in which we can find greater meaning and purpose. As discussed previously, many regular meditators find that a sense of compassion for others arises quite naturally. And research demonstrates that consciousness of others is better for our health than self-obsession.

Holocaust survivor and psychiatrist Viktor Frankl describes how finding meaning in life is one of the most important reasons to continue living. He also emphasizes the importance of looking beyond conventional self-aggrandizement:

Don't aim at success. The more you aim at it and make it a target, the more you are going to miss it. For success, like happiness, cannot be pursued; it must ensue, and it only does so as the unintended side effect of one's personal dedication to a cause greater than oneself or as the by-product of one's surrender to a person other than oneself.[20]

In essence: survivors tell us meditation helped heal them

The best way to find out about an unknown place is to talk to someone who's been there. That's the premise of apps such as TripAdvisor and Urbanspoon. If we're happy to benefit from the experience of others in matters as trivial as restaurant choice, how much more important is it to follow their advice when it comes to healing?

Survivors of serious illness consistently report that meditation—and thus mindfulness—is one of the most important things we can do to help ensure recovery.

Enough said.

Epilogue

There's a story I like about a New York merchant banker who goes on vacation to an idyllic seaside village in the Caribbean. After a few days observing life from the hotel deck, he makes his way down to the harbor mid-morning as the local fishermen finish cleaning their catch. The banker has seen how the local people live in rustic shanty homes near the beach. He's had a chance to observe their simple lifestyle. And being in the business of financial solutions, his mind has quite naturally turned to their situation.

Introducing himself to the bemused locals, he soon confirms his suspicions. Yes, the fishermen tell him, they go out every morning to fish, setting out around 6 a.m. and returning two or three hours later. Having sold their catch to a wholesaler, they then go home and spend the rest of the day relaxing with family and friends. In the evenings they enjoy dining together, usually downing a few home brews on the porch while watching the moon rise over the sea.

A gleam appears in the banker's eye as he explains he has a plan that can make them richer than they ever dared dream.

He gestures to a nearby bench and the fishermen sit around their unexpected visitor, curious to hear what he has to say.

If you were all to go out fishing twice a day instead of just the once, the banker begins, you'd immediately double your income. In a short space of time, you'd have collectively saved enough money to buy a bigger boat capable of traveling further and taking in much larger catches. The improved revenues could be ploughed back into the collective business, enabling the purchase of more such vessels until you possessed a whole fleet of them.

Some of the fishermen seem interested. Others have their reservations. As the banker glances about, one of the more excitable young men prompts him: "With bigger boats and more money, what will we do then?"

"Good question," replies the banker, going on to explain that the wholesaler to whom they sell their fish each day probably onsells the very same stock for two or three times the amount.

There's a rumble of assent that this, indeed, is the case.

What you do next, the banker explains, is cut out the wholesaler, buy your own refrigerator units, sell directly to buyers and immediately double or triple your collective income.

By now, every single one of the fishermen is keenly engaged. How could they not be?

Having won over his audience, the banker describes how the fishermen could systematically buy out every wholesaler on the island.

"What will we do then?" the same young fisherman asks, wondering if there could possibly be more.

The banker smoothly explains how the same business model can be replicated on surrounding islands. He talks about the benefits of economies of scale and building the fishing fleet into a sizeable operation. Mergers and acquisitions would propel growth further. And the more he talks, the more engaged the fishermen become, the young fisherman interjecting every so often "What will we do then?"

The banker continues, drawing to an inevitable conclusion. Once the company has achieved critical mass, he tells them, they can either exit by a private sale or go public with a stock market listing. Either way, the initial shareholders, including all the fishermen, can cash out. By the time they exit the deal, each of them will be worth millions.

The fishermen sit, digesting all this in stunned silence until, after a very long pause, one of the more thoughtful elders asks simply, "What will we do then?"

"Whatever the hell you want to do!" the banker is emphatic. "For starters, you won't have to work so hard, so you'll be able to spend most of the day doing exactly what you please. You can spend your time with family, kick back every night, have a few drinks with friends and enjoy your meal looking out at this great view . . ." It's only as he utters the last few words that the banker realizes what he's saying.

At the same moment the penny drops for every one of his audience. The old man nods. "What you're saying," he confirms, "is that we live like millionaires already."

There are a few reasons why I find this a delightful tale. At the most obvious level, it's a reminder to be grateful for the positive experiences we already enjoy. Mindfulness has an important part to play in this. If we're paying attention to the present moment, deliberately and nonjudgmentally, we're very much more likely to be happy than if we're caught up in mental agitation. This is even more true if our inner conversation tends to focus on the things we want but don't have, the people we're forced to spend time with but don't like, the life we long for but don't lead. By contrast, living in this moment, alert to what's actually occurring, is a very much likelier basis for contentment. As countless research studies suggest, it's also a more reliable basis for holistic good health.

The story also subtly points to the fallacy of a direct causal relationship between "out there" and "in here"—the superstition exposed through the ages by Buddha, Marcus Aurelius, Adam Smith, Tolstoy, and Albert Ellis, to name but a few, as well as any therapist when using cognitive behavior tools today. In seeking to change the fishermen's material circumstances, the banker is assuming a correlation between wealth and happiness. But this assumption is fundamentally flawed, as the banker should have known, living in a society that, although very much more affluent than that of the fishermen, is far from a haven of physical and psychological well-being.

But at its deepest level, we might see the story as a metaphor for mind itself. The merchant banker, so distracted by the compulsion to make money, has lost sight of the fact that its only use is what it can buy. What's the point of all the frenetic busy-ness and stress demanded by his master plan if the end result is a lifestyle little different qualitatively from the one the fishermen already enjoy?

It's our amazing good fortune that, like those fishermen, we're already the possessors of minds that are quite naturally radiant, lucid, and blissful. We don't need to engage in years of frenetic activity to manufacture or create such an outcome—it already exists. No amount of additional learning, intellectual gymnastics, or other cognitive activity is necessary or even relevant. The nature of our mind is already one of profound and abiding contentment. Our only task is to let go of the obstructing agitation and dullness that prevent us from realizing this, to tug aside the veil of cognition that separates us from the direct experience of our own primordial mind.

It's my heartfelt wish that this book has provided some useful guidance, techniques, and inspiration to help you realize this profound experience for yourself. I make no claims of originality for this synthesis of some of the wisdom and insights from which I have personally benefited. But I, along with the meditators with whom I share the journey, know that these teachings take us gently along a millennia-old pathway that leads to a direct encounter of the most transcendent kind— the experience, as revelatory as it is unexpected for most of us, of the abiding love and compassion that we discover is our own true nature.

Acknowledgements

My grateful thanks, first and foremost, to all those readers who have bought this and previous books. It's only your support that enables me to keep writing.

Thanks also to everyone involved in the publication of this book. Elizabeth Weiss and the whole team at Allen & Unwin have been staunch in their support for more than ten years; no author could wish for better. I am especially grateful to Matthew Lore, Sasha Tropp, and the team at The Experiment for your enthusiasm and support in taking this out to a much wider audience. I am also very grateful to Marg Sheehy, Susan Cameron, and Graham Tatnell for reading the manuscript; your feedback and insights have helped make it a more helpful book than it might otherwise have been. It is my partner at Organizational Mindfulness (OM), Clare Goodman, who transported me from temple to boardroom: without her unflagging enthusiasm, intellectual curiosity, and willingness to open doors, my experience and this book would be much narrower in scope.

My darling wife Koala is always unfailing in her encouragement of my writing, and was partly responsible for the title. When I returned from the gym one day and told her of my brainwave—"Why mindfulness is better than sex"—it was she who talked me down from that particular endorphin rush and convinced me that, for female readers in particular, "chocolate" may well be a more compelling proposition. Reluctant though I am to concede any point of argument to my wife, science proved her right!

But my most profound thanks of all go to my teacher Les Sheehy, director of the Tibetan Buddhist Society (TBS) here in Perth. For more than thirty years, Les has offered classes, week after week, to anyone with an interest in Tibetan Buddhism. He and his equally committed wife, Marg, have overseen the development of TBS in Perth from a handful of students in the lounge room of their house to the establishment of the only traditional Tibetan Buddhist temple in Western Australia—a truly amazing venue for increasingly well-attended classes and retreats.

Les chooses not to adopt a Tibetan name. He chooses not to write books. He chooses not to lead teaching tours to Europe or America. He shuns the limelight and would never accept one cent for his untiring work at the center. From the beginning, his motivation has only ever been to offer teachings as requested by his own teacher and the spiritual head of our organization, the peerless Geshe Acharya Thubten Loden.

Les's authenticity, humility, and devotion to his guru are as significant a teaching as the many profound insights he so powerfully—and often amusingly—conveys. His understanding is informed not only by ongoing study but also, more importantly, by direct meditative experience gained in private as well as through leading countless retreats. Les is a truly inspiring teacher whose eloquence in communicating the Dharma goes well beyond words, and the debt I owe him simply cannot be expressed.

May this book go some way to repaying Les's kindness, and help carry his life-changing wisdom into the hearts and minds of many readers.

Further reading

Alexander, E., *Proof of Heaven: A Neurosurgeon's Journey into the Afterlife*, Simon & Schuster, New York, 2012

Baumeister, R.F. & Tierney, J., *Willpower: Rediscovering the Greatest Human Strength*, Penguin Books, New York, 2011

Csikszentmihalyi, M., *Flow: The Psychology of Optimal Experience*, Harper Perennial Modern Classics, New York, 2008

Dalai Lama, His Holiness the & Berzin, A., *The Gelug/Kagyü Tradition of Mahamudra*, Snow Lion, Ithaca, New York, 1997

Gawler, I., *You Can Conquer Cancer: A New Way of Living*, revised edn, Michelle Anderson Publishing, Melbourne, 2013

Gilbert, D., *Stumbling on Happiness*, Vintage Books, New York, 2007

Gladwell, M., *Outliers: The Story of Success*, Little, Brown and Company, New York, 2008

McFarlane, T.J. (ed.), *Einstein and Buddha: The Parallel Sayings*, Ulysses Press, Berkeley, California, 2002

Rankin, L., *Mind Over Medicine: Scientific Proof That You Can Heal Yourself*, Hay House, Carlsbad, California, 2013

Ricard, M. & Trinh, X.T., *The Quantum and the Lotus: A Journey to the Frontiers Where Science and Buddhism Meet*, Three Rivers Press, New York, 2001

Seligman, M., *Flourish: A Visionary New Understanding of Happiness and Well-being*, Free Press, New York, 2011

Stone, M., *The Inner Tradition of Yoga: A Guide to Yoga Philosophy for the Contemporary Practitioner*, Shambhala, Boston, 2008

van Lommel, P., *Consciousness Beyond Life: The Science of the Near-Death Experience*, HarperOne, New York, 2010

Wallace, B.A., *Minding Closely: The Four Applications of Mindfulness*, Snow Lion, Ithaca, New York, 2011

Notes

Chapter 1: Is mindfulness really better than chocolate?

1 See S. Bradt, "Wandering mind not a happy mind," *Harvard Gazette*, November 11, 2010, http://news.harvard.edu/gazette /story/2010/11/wandering-mind-not-a-happy-mind, accessed May 24, 2013.

2 J. Watson, "Meditating Marines: Military tries mindfulness to lower stress," NBC News, January 20, 2013, http://vitals. nbcnews.com/_news/2013/01/20/16612244-meditating-marines-military-tries-mindfulness-to-lower-stress, accessed March 26, 2014.

Chapter 2: What is mindfulness and why does it matter?

1 The essence of the Four Noble Truths may be summarized as: The existence of dissatisfaction; the causes of dissatisfaction; the end of dissatisfaction; how to achieve the end of dissatisfaction.

Chapter 3: How to meditate

1 J. Hirshfield, "Spiritual Poetry: 22 poems about spirituality and enlightenment," Poetry Foundation, June 28, 2006, www .poetryfoundation.org/article/178390, accessed July 5, 2013.

Chapter 4: The benefits of meditation and mindfulness

1 This increase was noted by University of Oregon psychologist Michael Posner and Yi-Yuan Tang of Texas Tech University in an editorial to *SCAN* (*Social Cognitive and Affective Neuroscience*).

See "Mindfulness meditation heightens a listener's musical engagement," Science News, *Science Daily*, January 30, 2013, www.sciencedaily.com/releases/2013/01/130130132415.htm, accessed May 8, 2013.

2 G. Desbordes, et al., "Effects of mindful-attention and compassion meditation training on amygdala response to emotional stimuli in an ordinary, non-meditative state," *Frontiers in Human Neuroscience*, November 1, 2012, vol. 6, article no. 292, www.frontiersin.org/human_neuroscience/10.3389/fnhum .2012.00292/abstract, accessed April 29, 2013.

3 M. Murphy & S. Donovan, *The Physical and Psychological Effects of Meditation: A review of contemporary research with a comprehensive bibliography, 1931–1996*, 2nd edn, Institute of Noetic Sciences, Petaluma, California, 1997.

4 See also: Jon Kabat-Zinn, *Full Catastrophe Living: Using the Wisdom of Your Body and Mind to Face Stress, Pain, and Illness*, revised edn, Bantam Books, New York, 2013.

5 See "Overview of the Shamatha Project," UC Davis Center for Mind and Brain, http://mindbrain.ucdavis.edu/labs/Saron /shamatha-project, accessed April 29, 2013.

6 "Research Is In: Meditation Is Good For Cellular Health," News and Research, UC Davis College of Letters and Science, www.ls.ucdavis.edu/dss/news-and-research/shamatha-project-nov10.html, accessed November 20, 2013.

7 E. Epel, et al., "Can meditation slow rate of cellular aging? Cognitive stress, mindfulness, and telomeres," *Annals of the New York Academy of Sciences*, August 2009, vol. 1172, pp. 34–53, www.ncbi.nlm.nih.gov/pmc/articles/PMC3057175, accessed November 20, 2013.

8   R.K. Wallace et al., "The effects of the transcendental meditation and TM-Sidhi program on the aging process," *International Journal of Neuroscience*, February 1982, vol. 16, no. 1, pp. 53–8.

9   Information on DHEA from studies presented by I. Greenwell, "DHEA and Anti-Aging Medicine," *Life Extension* magazine, June 2002, http://www.encognitive.com/files/DHEA%20 AND%20ANTI-AGING%20MEDICINE.pdf, accessed April 29, 2013. See also the information on the Project Meditation website, www.project-meditation.org/community/learn -how-you-can-benefit-project-meditation/26-longevity-bene ficial-hormones-released-during-meditation.html, accessed April 29, 2013.

10 R. Herron & S. Hillis, "The Impact of the Transcendental Meditation Program on Government Payments to Physicians in Quebec: An Update," *American Journal of Health Promotion*, May–June 2000, vol. 14, no. 5, pp. 284–91, http://ajhpcontents. org/doi/abs/10.4278/0890-1171-14.5.284, accessed April 30, 2013.

11 D. Schoormans & I. Nyklicek, "Mindfulness and psychologic well-being: are they related to type of meditation technique practiced?," *Journal of Alternative and Complementary Medicine*, July 2011, vol. 17, no. 7, pp. 629–34. See www.positivehealth .com/research/schoormans-and-nyklicek, accessed May 20, 2013.

12 J. Kabat-Zinn, et al., "Four-Year Follow-Up of a Meditation-Based Program for the Self-Regulation of Chronic Pain: Treatment Outcomes and Compliance," *Clinical Journal of Pain*, 1986, vol. 2, no. 3, pp. 159–73, http://journals.lww.com

/clinicalpain/Abstract/1986/02030/Four_Year_Follow_Up _of_a_Meditation_Based_Program.4.aspx, accessed April 30, 2013.

13 See F. Zeidan et al., "Brain Mechanisms Supporting the Modulation of Pain by Mindfulness Meditation," *The Journal of Neuroscience*, April 6, 2011, vol. 31, no. 14, pp. 5540–8, www .jneurosci.org/content/31/14/5540.full.pdf, accessed March 26, 2014.

14 See S. Boyles, "Brain Imaging Shows Impact of Brief Mindfulness Meditation Training," April 6, 2011, www.medicinenet .com/script/main/art.asp?articlekey=142816, accessed May 20, 2013.

15 R. Schneider, et al., "Long-Term Effects of Stress Reduction on Mortality in Persons ≥55 Years of Age With Systemic Hypertension," *The American Journal of Cardiology*, 2005, vol. 5, www.ajconline.org/article/S0002-9149(05)00183-9/abstract, accessed April 30, 2013.

16 C.N. Alexander, et al., "Transcendental meditation, mindfulness, and longevity: an experimental study with the elderly," *Journal of Personality and Social Psychology*, December 1989, vol. 57, no. 6, pp. 950–64.

17 J. Ladwig, "Mindfulness meditation may relieve chronic inflammation," University of Wisconsin-Madison News, January 16, 2013, www.news.wisc.edu/21428, accessed April 30, 2013.

18 See S. Bernstein, "Ease Arthritis Symptoms with meditation: mindfulness and meditation empower people to deal with the pain and stress of arthritis," Arthritis Foundation, www.arthritis today.org/arthritis-treatment/natural-and-alternative-treatments

/meditation-and-relaxation/meditation-eases-symptoms.php, accessed May 20, 2013.

19 See E. Camus, "Once dismissed as pretentious but now brain scans prove Eastern philosophies can be effective in treating mental illness," *Daily Mail*, July 26, 2012, www.dailymail .co.uk/health/article-2103095/Once-dismissed-pretentious-brain-scans-prove-Eastern-philosophies-effective-treating-mental-illness.html, accessed April 30, 2013.

20 See M. Wheeler, "Meditation reduces loneliness," UCLA Newsroom, August 14, 2012, http://newsroom.ucla.edu/portal/ucla /meditation-reduces-loneliness-237463.aspx, accessed April 30, 2013.

21 See "Press Release: Mindfulness Meditation Reduces Loneliness in Older Adults, Carnegie Mellon Study Shows," Carnegie Mellon News, July 24, 2012, www.cmu.edu/news /stories/archives/2012/july/july24_meditationstudy.html, accessed January 15, 2014

22 See www.huffingtonpost.com/2012/08/07/thich-nhat-hanh-quotes _n_1753088.html, accessed January 15, 2014

23 See "Better Living Through Mindfulness: U Study Connects Traits of Mindfulness to Emotional Well-Being," U News Center, University of Utah, March 23, 2013, http://unews .utah.edu/news_releases/better-living-through-mindfulness, accessed April 30, 2013.

24 See L. Cohen, et al., "Psychological adjustment and sleep quality in a randomized trial of the effects of a Tibetan yoga intervention in patients with lymphoma," *Cancer*, May 15, 2004, vol. 100, no. 10, pp. 2253–60, http://www.ncbi.nlm

.nih.gov/pubmed/15139072, accessed April 30, 2013, and W.B. Britton et al., "Polysomnographic and subjective profiles of sleep continuity before and after mindfulness-based cognitive therapy in partially remitted depression," *Psychosomatic Medicine*, July–August 2010, vol. 72, no. 6, pp. 539–48, http://www.ncbi.nlm.nih.gov/pubmed/20467003, accessed April 30, 2013.

25 See the work of Tibetan Bon lama Tenzin Wangyal Rinpoche, *The Tibetan Yogas of Dream and Sleep*, Snow Lion, Ithaca, New York, 1998.

26 Stephen LaBerge, *Lucid Dreaming: A Concise Guide to Awakening in Your Dreams and in Your Life*, Sounds True, Inc., Boulder, Colorado, 2004, p. 14.

27 Elizabeth A. Stanley et al., "Mindfulness-based Mind Fitness Training: A Case Study of a High-Stress Predeployment Military Cohort," *Cognitive and Behavioral Practice*, November 2010, vol. 8, no. 4, pp. 566–76, www.sciencedirect.com/science/article/pii/S1077722911000083, accessed May 3, 2013.

28 See K. Neff, "Self-Compassion: A Healthier Way of Relating to Yourself," www.self-compassion.org, accessed August 19, 2013.

29 Michael Chaskalson, *The Mindful Workplace: Developing Resilient Individuals and Resonant Organizations with MBSR*, John Wiley & Sons, London, 2011, p. 118.

30 See "Lose weight your way: 9,000 readers rate 13 diet plans and tools," *Consumer Reports*, February 2013, www.consumerreports.org/cro/magazine/2013/02/lose-weight-your-way/index.htm, accessed July 10, 2013.

31 S. Bowen, et al., "Mindfulness Meditation and Substance Use in an Incarcerated Population," *Psychology of Addictive Behaviors*, 2006, vol. 20, no. 3, pp. 343–7, www.prison.dhamma.org /en/na/NRF Substance Abuse Study 2006.pdf, accessed May 2, 2013.

32 See "Mindfulness meditation heightens a listener's musical engagement," Science Daily, January 30, 2013, www.science daily.com/releases/2013/01/130130132415.htm, accessed May 8, 2013.

33 See "Brief Mindfulness Training May Boost Test Scores, Working Memory," press release, Association for Psychological Science, March 26, 2013, www.psychologicalscience .org/index.php/news/releases/brief-mindfulness-train ing-may-boost-test-scores-working-memory.html, accessed May 2, 2013.

34 D. Goleman, "The Lama in the Lab," in *Destructive Emotions: How Can We Overcome Them?*, Bantam Books, London, 2003, pp. 3–27.

35 N. Doidge, *The Brain That Changes Itself: Stories of Personal Triumph from the Frontiers of Brain Science*, Scribe, Melbourne, 2008.

36 See M. Kaufman, "Meditation Gives Brain a Charge, Study Finds," *Washington Post*, January 3, 2005, www.washingtonpost.com /wp-dyn/articles/A43006-2005Jan2.html, accessed May 24, 2013.

37 Andy Fraser (ed.), *The Healing Power of Meditation*, Shambhala, Boston, 2013.

Chapter 5: How mindfulness benefits organizations

1   B. Oshry, *Seeing Systems: Unlocking the Mysteries of Organizational Life*, Berret-Kohler, San Francisco, 2007.

2   R. Boyatzis & A. McKee, *Mindfulness: An Essential Element of Resonant Leadership*, Harvard Business School Press, Boston, 2005, p. 17.

3   See A. Gorlick, "Media multitaskers pay mental price, Stanford study shows," *Stanford Report*, August 24, 2009, http://news.stanford.edu/news/2009/august24/multitask-research-study-082409.html, accessed August 13, 2013.

4   See "The Myth of Multitasking," National Public Radio, May 10, 2013, www.npr.org/2013/05/10/182861382/the-myth-of-multitasking, accessed August 13, 2013.

5   Boyatzis & McKee, *Mindfulness*, p. 18.

6   See Circadian Technologies, "Absenteeism: The Bottom-Line Killer," 2005, www.workforceinstitute.org/wp-content/themes/revolution/docs/Absenteeism-Bottom-Line.pdf.

7   Mental Health Foundation, *Mindfulness Report 2010*, Mental Health Foundation, London, 2010.

8   See "What are the financial benefits?," iOpener Institute, www.iopenerinstitute.com/what-are-the-financial-benefits.aspx?lang=en, accessed August 14, 2013.

9   Chaskalson, *The Mindful Workplace*, p. 4.

10 See D. Gelles, "The mind business," *FT Magazine*, August 24, 2014, www.ft.com/intl/cms/s/2/d9cb7940-ebea-11e1-985a-00144feab49a.html#axzz2SafbMJhR, accessed May 7, 2013.

11 See F. Coleman, "Mindfulness: An Ancient Skill for Thriving in the Modern Innovation Economy," *Huffington Post*, March

28, 2013, www.huffingtonpost.com/flynn-coleman/mindful
ness-an-ancient_b_2957970.html, accessed August 14, 2013.

12 See Coleman, "Mindfulness."

13 Annie McKee, et al., *Becoming a Resonant Leader: Develop Your Emotional Intelligence, Renew Your Relationships, Sustain Your Effectiveness*, Harvard Business School Press, Boston, 2008.

14 M. Carroll, *The Mindful Leader: Ten Principles for Bringing Out the Best in Ourselves and Others*, Trumpeter Books, Boston, 2007, p. 18.

Chapter 6: Ten tips for getting into the meditation habit

1 For more about this remarkable lady or to support the nunnery she has established in India, see www.tenzinpalmo.com, accessed May 13, 2013.

2 See A. Molloy, "What a difference a month makes," *Canberra Times*, April 19, 2013, www.canberratimes.com.au/lifestyle /life/what-a-difference-a-month-makes-20130419-2i54u.html, accessed May 13, 2013.

3 See Molloy, "What a difference a month makes."

4 R.F. Baumeister & J. Tierney, *Willpower: Rediscovering the Greatest Human Strength*, Penguin Books, New York, 2011, p. 244.

5 G.A.T. Loden, *Path to Enlightenment in Tibetan Buddhism*, Tushita Publications, Melbourne, 1993, p. 136.

Chapter 7: How to apply mindfulness in your daily life

1 T. Schwartz, "How to Be Mindful in an 'Unmanageable' World," Harvard Business Review Blog Network, February 27, 2013, http://blogs.hbr.org/2013/02/how-to-be-mind ful-in-an-un mana, accessed November 29, 2013.

Chapter 8: Our mindfulness journey

1   N. Qubein, "Creating Your Own Future," Nido Qubein website, www.nidoqubein.com/articledisplay.cfm?aid=30, accessed November 29, 2013.

2   The Dalai Lama, *Words of Wisdom: Selected Quotes from His Holiness the Dalai Lama*, Margaret Gee, Sydney, 1992, p. 49.

3   See K. Anders Ericsson et al., "The Role of Deliberate Practice in the Acquisition of Expert Performance," *Psychological Review*, 1993, vol. 100, no. 3, pp. 363–406, http://graphics8 .nytimes.com/images/blogs/freakonomics/pdf/Deliberate Practice%28PsychologicalReview%29.pdf, accessed March 26, 2014.

4   M. Gladwell, *Outliers: The Story of Success*, Little, Brown and Company, New York, 2008, p. 35.

5   D.J. Levitin, *This Is Your Brain on Music: The Science of a Human Obsession*, Dutton, New York, 2006, p. 197.

6   M. Gladwell, *Outliers,* p. 35.

Chapter 9: How mindfulness makes us happier

1   See www.econlib.org/library/Smith/smMS4.html, accessed January 15, 2014.

2   Aristotle, *Nichomachean Ethics*, see "Aristotle," *The Pursuit of Happiness* blog, www.pursuit-of-happiness.org/history-of-happiness/aristotle, accessed November 11, 2013.

3   See www.forbes.com/sites/jacquelynsmith/2013/03/22/the-happiest-and-unhappiest-jobs-in-america, accessed January 15, 2014.

4   R. Frank, *Luxury Fever: Weighing the Cost of Excess*, Princeton University Press, New Jersey, 2010.

5   See www.psychologytoday.com/blog/how-happiness/201202
     /does-marriage-make-us-happy-should-it, accessed January 15,
     2014.

6   See http://en.wikipedia.org/wiki/Coolidge_effect, accessed
     January 15, 2014.

7   D. Gilbert, *Stumbling on Happiness*, Harper Perennial,
     London, 2006, p. 220.

8   Gilbert, *Stumbling on Happiness*, p. 217.

9   M. Aurelius, *Meditations*, Chapter 8, verse 47, Internet Classics
     Archive, http://classics.mit.edu/Antoninus/meditations.8.eight.
     html, accessed January 15, 2014.

10   See "Ellis' Irrational Beliefs," Changing Minds, http://changing
     minds.org/explanations/belief/irrational_beliefs.htm, accessed
     June 13, 2013.

Chapter 10: What is mind?

1   S. Kierkegaard, *Works of Love*, trans. Howard V. Hong, Harper
     & Row, New York, 1963, p. 23.

2   R. Descartes, *Selected Philosophical Writings*, trans. John
     Cottingham et al., Cambridge University Press, Cambridge,
     1988, p. 36.

3   M. Stone, *The Inner Tradition of Yoga: A Guide to Yoga Philo-
     sophy for the Contemporary Practitioner*, Shambhala, Boston,
     p. 68.

4   D. Kennedy & C. Norman, "What We Don't Know," *Science*,
     2005, vol. 309, no. 5731, p. 75.

5   See www.sbinstitute.com/sites/default/files/matofgaps.pdf,
     accessed January 15, 2014.

6   F. Crick, *The Astonishing Hypothesis*, Scribner, New York, 1994, p. 3.

7   B.A. Wallace, *Minding Closely: The Four Applications of Mindfulness*, Snow Lion, Ithaca, New York, 2011, p. 110.

8   P. van Lommel, *Consciousness Beyond Life: The Science of the Near-Death Experience*, HarperOne, New York, 2011.

9   P. van Lommel et al., "Near-death experiences in survivors of cardiac arrest: a prospective study in the Netherlands," *Lancet*, 2001, vol. 358, pp. 2039–45.

10   E. Alexander, *Proof of Heaven: A Neurosurgeon's Journey into the Afterlife*, Macmillan, Sydney, 2012, p. 8.

11   Alexander, *Proof of Heaven*, p. 153.

12   See http://en.wikiquote.org/wiki/Albert_Abraham_Michelson, accessed January 15, 2014.

13   W. Heisenberg, *Physics and Beyond: Encounters and Conversations*, trans. A.J. Pomerans, Harper & Row, New York, 1971, p. 206.

14   Quoted in T.J. McFarlane (ed.), *Einstein and Buddha: The Parallel Sayings*, Ulysses Press, Berkeley, California, 2002, p. 99.

15   Quoted in T.J. McFarlane (ed.), *Einstein and Buddha*, p. 126.

16   Quoted in T.J. McFarlane (ed.), *Einstein and Buddha,* p. 69.

17   W. Nisker, "Introduction," in McFarlane (ed.), *Einstein and Buddha*, p. vii.

18   This is a widely accepted definition of conventional mind. The word "awareness" is sometimes substituted for "cognition," but its meaning in this context is the same.

19   D. Goddard (ed.), *A Buddhist Bible*, Beacon Press, Boston, 1970, p. 283.

20 E. Schrödinger, *What Is Life? With Mind and Matter*, Cambridge University Press, Cambridge, 2012, p. 132.

21 M. Ricard & X.T. Trinh, *The Quantum and the Lotus: A Journey to the Frontiers Where Science and Buddhism Meet*, Three Rivers Press, New York, 2001, p. 270.

Chapter 11: How to meditate on your own mind

1 The Dalai Lama & A. Berzin, *The Gelug/Kagyü Tradition of Mahamudra*, Snow Lion, Ithaca, New York, 1997, p. 139.

2 B.A. Wallace, *Minding Closely: The Four Applications of Mindfulness*, Snow Lion, Ithaca, New York, 2011, p. 61.

3 T. Nhat Hanh, *The Miracle of Mindfulness: An Introduction to the Practice of Meditation*, Beacon Press, Boston, 1975, p. 42.

4 Dalai Lama & Berzin, *The Gelug/Kagyü Tradition of Mahamudra*, p. 141.

5 Wallace, *Minding Closely*, p. 215.

6 Wallace, *Minding Closely*, p. 109.

7 S. Batchelor, *Confession of a Buddhist Atheist*, Spiegel & Grau, New York, 2010, p. 133.

8 See www.keithdowman.net/mahamudra/tilopa.htm.

9 Dalai Lama & Berzin, *The Gelug/Kagyü Tradition of Mahamudra*, p. 303.

10 Dalai Lama & Berzin, *The Gelug/Kagyü Tradition of Mahamudra*, p. 288.

Chapter 12: Healing and the mind

1 Quoted in N. Cousins, *Anatomy of an Illness*, Norton, New York, 1980, pp. 68–9.

2 L. Rankin, *Mind Over Medicine: Scientific Proof That You Can Heal Yourself*, Hay House, Carlsbad, California, 2013, p. xiv.

3   B.H. Lipton, *The Biology of Belief: Unleashing the Power of Consciousness, Matter and Miracles*, Hay House, Carlsbad, California, 2008, p. 32.

4   See www.theguardian.com/science/2013/jun/02/twins-identical-genes-different-health-study, accessed January 15, 2014.

5   M. Gladwell, *Outliers: The Story of Success*, Little, Brown and Company, New York, 2008.

6   Gladwell, *Outliers*, p. 3.

7   See C. Hassed, 'The health benefits of meditation and being mindful," Monash University, Melbourne, 2012, www.49.com.au/wp-content/uploads/The-health-benefits-of-meditation-and-being-mindful_v21-2.pdf, accessed July 26, 2013.

8   Rankin, *Mind Over Medicine*, p. 94.

9   See www.onthepage.org/outsiders/should_you_bowl_alone.htm, accessed January 15, 2014.

10 Rankin, *Mind Over Medicine*, p. 124.

11 See N. Crawford, "Positivity pays off for winners of psychology's top monetary prize," American Psychological Association, www.apa.org/monitor/julaug02/positivity.aspx, accessed July 29, 2013.

12 D. Michie, *Enlightenment to Go: The Classic Buddhist Path of Compassion and Transformation*, Allen & Unwin, Sydney, 2010.

13 A. Einstein, *The World As I See It*, Carol Publishing Group, Secaucus, New Jersey, 1999.

14 See www.psychiatrictimes.com/articles/antidepressants-versus-placebos-meaningful-advantages-are-lacking, accessed January 15, 2014.

15 J.B. Moseley, et al., "A Controlled Trial of Arthroscopic Surgery for Osteoarthritis of the Knee," *New England Journal of Medicine*, July 2002, vol. 347, pp. 81–8, www.nejm.org/doi/full/10.1056/NEJMoa013259, accessed November 23, 2013.

16 T.J. Kaptchuk, et al., "Components of placebo effect: randomised controlled trial in patients with irritable bowel syndrome," *British Medical Journal*, May 2008, vol. 336, no. 7651, pp. 999–1003, www.bmj.com/content/336/7651/999, accessed November 23, 2013.

17 See www.nytimes.com/1988/06/28/science/probing-the-enigma-of-multiple-personality.html?pagewanted=all&src=pm, accessed January 15, 2014.

18 I. Gawler, *You Can Conquer Cancer: A New Way of Living*, revised edn, Michelle Anderson Publishing, Melbourne, 2013, p. 11.

19 J. Kabat-Zinn, "Mindfulness-Based Intervention in Medicine and Psychiatry: What Does It Mean to Be 'Mindfulness-Based'?", in A. Fraser (ed.), *The Healing Power of Meditation: Leading Experts on Buddhism, Psychology, and Medicine Explore the Health Benefits of Contemplative Practice*, Shambhala, Boston, 2013, pp. 93–119.

20 See http://en.wikiquote.org/wiki/Man%27s_Search_for_Meaning, accessed January 15, 2014.

About the author

....

DAVID MICHIE is an internationally published writer and meditation coach. He is the author of numerous books, including *Hurry Up and Meditate, Buddhism for Busy People, Enlightenment to Go*, and a series of novels featuring the Dalai Lama's cat.

Michie teaches mindfulness and meditation techniques to a wide variety of audiences, and has developed guided meditations to benefit both secular and Buddhist practitioners. The cofounder of Organisational Mindfulness, which caters to the corporate sector, Michie is a student of the Tibetan Buddhist Society and lives in Perth, Australia. Please visit www.david-michie.com for more information.